LOTHIAN
AUSTRALIAN
garden
SERIES

Beautiful gardens with less water

Series Editor
John Patrick

John Patrick

A LOTHIAN BOOK

Acknowledgements

The enthusiasm and drive for this book originated with Melbourne Water, most notably with Alan Fleming with whom I discussed the need for this book at the Landscape Australia Conference in 1994. I acknowledge his unstinting enthusiasm and help, together with that of Paul Orfanos of Melbourne Water. Kevin Connelly expedited his foreword with good humour and his usual enthusiasm for the cause of water conservation.

Dr Peter May of the Victorian College of Agriculture & Horticulture at Burnley gave balanced judgement and comment on the draft manuscript, and I was further aided by discussion with Stephen Forbes, Barrie Gallacher, Michael Looker, Paul Thompson and Rodger Elliot.

My wife Bridget typed the manuscript, long and tiresome as it was, and Beryl Hill worked tirelessly through several family traumas to edit my over-enthusiastic writing to the required length. As usual with this series, Julia McLeish produced her drawings with alacrity and skill.

Paul Harker at the Meteorological Office, London, was exemplary in his rapid response to my call for assistance.

I thank them all for their help in completing this book.

A Lothian Book
Thomas C. Lothian Pty Ltd
11 Munro Street, Port Melbourne
Victoria 3207

Copyright © John Patrick 1994
Copyright © illustrations Thomas C. Lothian Pty Ltd 1994
First published 1994

National Library of Australia
Cataloguing-in-publication data:

Patrick, John, 1951– .
    Beautiful gardens with less water

    Bibliography.
    Includes index.
    ISBN 0 85091 657 7

    1. Landscape gardening — Water conservation — Australia. I. Title. (Series: Lothian Australian garden series).

635.0994

Cover design by David Constable
Illustrations by Julia McLeish
Typeset in Cheltenham and Rockwell by Bookset Pty Ltd
Printed in Australia by Impact Printing

Foreword

The topic of this book is very timely. Many Australian cities, like Melbourne, are rapidly approaching the crossroads in respect of their future water supplies. With domestic water consumption rising faster than the number of households the two viable options are clear — reduce consumption, or divert another river into our dams within the next eight to ten years, a very short time given the complex planning and community consultation issues involved.

The current user-pays approach to water charging has effected some reduction in usage, but there are limits. So can we reduce consumption further? Domestic consumption is over half the total annual water usage, and gardening accounts for about 40 per cent of domestic usage, thus offering the greatest potential for reduction.

But we have been brought up on the traditional English approach, which is very thirsty for water. Is this really appropriate for our conditions? What are the alternatives? John Patrick shows us how to have a beautiful garden, yet significantly reduce water consumption, and even help lower our water bill. He explains in simple terms and with excellent illustrations the principles, planning and the 'how to' involved. It is an exciting new approach to gardening, written in an easy-to-read style by a most experienced garden specialist.

KEVIN CONNELLY
Chairman (1992–93)
Melbourne Water Resources Review

is a registered trademark of Melbourne Water Corporation. Melbourne Water Xeriscape has assisted in the publication of this book.

Contents

Introduction

Water is essential to all life on earth. All living creatures, even those that have adapted to survival in the world's driest environments, require water to survive. Humans are no exception to this: we need water to drink, for industry, food production and cleaning.

Our media broadcasts emphasise the effects of water shortages with graphic scenes of victims of civil war or natural catastrophes in desperate need of unpolluted water. Drought years in different parts of Australia led to devastating effects for urban and rural dwellers alike through the loss of stock and crops, the difficulties of daily life with limited water, and the attendant problems of fire.

In many other parts of the world water is in critically short supply. Water shortages can be tolerated by natural systems. Plants, for example, have a number of ways of minimising their demand for water, and they can survive droughts. Animals and birds, too, have adapted to their environment: on occasions their numbers may be decimated, but generally recover once the drought is over. Major problems arise, however, when human populations increase to levels that cannot be sustained by existing water resources.

We continually modify our environment, bringing about major changes to the water pattern. Increased urbanisation with its pavements and buildings leads to more rapid drainage, so that water is lost from the environment. This reduces the humidity of the atmosphere, increases the temperature because of the lack of evaporation, and reduces soil water available to plants, all of which increase the effects of drought on plants. To make matters worse, in place of native trees, shrubs and grasses, tolerant of the existing climate, we demand lush garden schemes of lawns and ornamental plantings that need improved soil conditions, the addition of fertilisers and volumes of water to ensure satisfactory growth.

Our demand for water is such that in periods of drought we simply cannot meet demand. Furthermore, as the population increases this demand for water increases. Availability of water will eventually be the limiting factor to population growth in Australia.

Much of the water demand of urban areas is created by industry, but domestic consumption represents about 52 per cent of water consumption, and is currently increasing by 2.8 per cent each year.

As a result, we must construct more dams. While the number of potential sites for dams is finite, by building more dams we reduce natural habitats for plants and animals, lose remote landscape, and a considerable cost has to be borne by the community. In times of water shortage, industry would have to reduce production and working hours, partly because of decreased demand,

Domestic water use

The total water demand for a city like Melbourne has increased from about 50 gigalitres in 1890 to well in excess of 400 gigalitres in 1990, an increase of nearly 3 per cent a year.

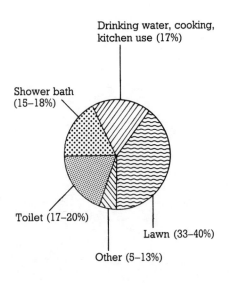

Drinking water, cooking, kitchen use (17%)

Shower bath (15–18%)

Toilet (17–20%)

Lawn (33–40%)

Other (5–13%)

partly because there would be inadequate water to service the demands of industry.

Major savings in water demand can be made without affecting our lifestyles in any detrimental way. All that is required is some modification of our attitudes and our expectations.

Half of the water we use on gardens could be saved by using it more efficiently, without any noticeable changes to the appearance of our towns and cities. In part we use enormous amounts of water because we fail to recognise the character of our environment. Many of our gardening books are English in origin, and influence us to create gardens that are quite unrealistic for our environment. In spite of our best efforts and the ongoing application of water, our gardens of exotic plants do not match the splendour of the same plants grown in England.

Australians can still have beautiful gardens, but we must modify our approach to gardening by recognising the characteristics of our environment, and by creating different, less water-dependent gardens.

We do not live in the lush and fertile landscape of northern Europe (especially England); we live in a dry continent, and must accept that the social cost of continuing our current approach to gardening will be enormous. Changing our attitude can result in gardens of rich beauty that may be the envy of the English, who can only grow these plants indoors.

By following practices outlined in this book, by applying the design principles and understanding something of the way in which plants use and save water, you will be able to make a very real contribution to our community. Many of these changes will not be hard. Most of you have already begun to apply low-water principles by growing many of the low-water plants that I will be recommending.

The seven key steps in the process of designing, creating and maintaining water-saving gardens are:
- planning and designing the garden for local conditions and microclimates
- careful analysis and improvement of soils
- practical lawn areas (the most water-demanding of all)
- choosing appropriate plants
- designing efficient watering systems
- mulching
- appropriate maintenance.

Landscapes created using these principles are called Xeriscapes — beautiful gardens using less water.

French gardens

The delightful gardens of Provence in southern France were created where water is a scarce commodity, where summers are dry and soils are porous. The increased gentrification of this beautiful area has resulted in more swimming pools, and a resultant shortage of water for traditional agriculture. If this process continues there will be a fundamental change in the character of this rural landscape. Australian tourists do not return bemoaning the harshness of these gardens or lack of greenness; they praise the gardens of this particular climate.

Because of the Garden of St Erth's remote location, these cottage-garden plants must be able to tolerate low water levels and, when conditions are really dry, to survive on their own.

Climate — its relevance to your garden

Did you know?

More than 50 per cent of Australia is desert, and less than 30 per cent of the rest receives sufficient rainfall to support general agriculture; 50 per cent receives less than 300 mm.

Regional variations

In July 1994 weather conditions were such that Western Australia received heavy rainfall, while much of the south-east of Australia experienced prolonged periods of drought.

Similarly in New Zealand, Auckland has been experiencing an extended drought over a number of years, resulting in nearly empty reservoirs and restrictions to protect water resources — the use of hoses and outdoor taps will be banned during the whole of next summer.

Australia is the driest settled continent in the world, with great year-to-year rainfall variations. Australia's climate is diverse, ranging from the alpine areas of the south-east to the tropical areas of the north, to the areas of little or no rainfall in central Australia.

Water demands of gardens relate to the amount of rainfall, as well as its distribution through the year. Much of coastal Australia, where most of the population lives, has more annual rainfall than London.

Much of the rainfall in towns and cities is lost for use by plants. Not only have we paved and built over much of the soil surface, the remaining areas have become so compacted that water is slow to penetrate. To make matters worse, we have to contend with increased surface drainage and evaporation.

In northern Australia most rain falls in tropical summer storms, while in the south winter rainfalls predominate. In the sub-tropical areas between (such as Sydney) there is a double rainfall peak.

Evaporation exceeds rainfall in most of Australia. Evaporation varies from year to year, and place to place, and depends on temperature, humidity and sunshine. The higher the temperature, the higher the evaporation rate will be, though this also depends upon the humidity of the atmosphere — evaporation is reduced where humidity is high, and also depends on the number of hours of sunshine. Where evaporation matches rainfall lush green rainforest flourishes in the relatively moist, humid conditions. Where conditions are dry (e.g. in central Australia), the evaporation rate may be eighteen times the rainfall.

Evaporation rates give you a useful basis for calculating water application rates to replace the water lost by plants through evaporation and transpiration (that is, evapotranspiration). This varies according to the type of plant being cultivated; plants transpire water at varying rates.

As humidity (the amount of water vapour in an air mass) falls and the atmosphere becomes drier plants transpire more water, though many plants have ways to reduce transpiration (see pp. 21–7). Humidity is generally higher where air blows off the sea, so that westerly winds in Perth or south-westerly winds in Melbourne are generally quite humid and often carry rain, while those from hot inland areas (easterly winds in Perth, northerlies in Melbourne) are dry. For plants that cannot adapt to dry environments these dry winds are very damaging; the plants have no means of controlling water loss and rapidly become stressed. Sometimes a few days of extremely dry, hot weather can cause more significant damage to plants than a longer period of low rainfall.

Australia is on the equivalent latitude as southern USA, India, north Africa and Mexico; it shows many similar climatic characteristics (e.g. low rainfall and high solar energy).

Had the first European settlers been Spanish, Portuguese or Moroccans, with their tradition of living in dry, hot climates, our gardens might have been better suited to the Australian environment.

Drought

So far I have referred to 'normal' years, but Australia's climate reflects cyclical patterns. Prolonged periods without rain create drought conditions, sometimes localised, at other times more widespread.

Drought is a 'lack of sufficient water to meet normal requirements'. Australia experiences a drought approximately every ten years. In part this results from El Niño, the seasonal warming of water off the South American coast.

In many regions drought is likely to be the limiting factor. The average conditions in much of our coastal residential strip allows us to grow an extensive range of plants, but we tend to include in our gardens many plants ill-suited to our rainfall and humidity. To keep them alive through many summers, we use valuable water resources. We should accept that plants need some assistance for survival through micro-climates and drip irrigation, that some of our chosen plants are unsuitable, and that others will be lost in drought.

Changes in climate

Not all places in larger areas (meso-climates) have similar climates: in intermediate (middle) areas, coastal areas are different from inland areas, while changes in altitude also have an impact. Changes can occur over quite small distances.

It is important to note these changes, both in terms of your own garden and in terms of the origin of plants. It is not sufficient to suggest that, because a plant originates in California, it will automatically thrive in our hot, dry summers — it may originate high in the mountains (the Sierra Nevada), where conditions are considerably cooler and may be wetter than the coastal plains

El Niño

This occurs about every three to eight years, and has widespread effects: increased wet periods in some areas (south-eastern USA, western and south-eastern South America and the Pacific), warmer periods in Alaska and western and eastern Canada, and dry conditions in Australia and south-east Asia, as well as south-east Africa and western South America. Australia is only one part of a world climatic system.

Rarely is Australia considered in the context of world climates: it occupies a corresponding position in the Southern Hemisphere to many of the driest parts of the Northern Hemisphere. The intensity of the sun demands that we wear a hat, a shirt and sunscreen when gardening!

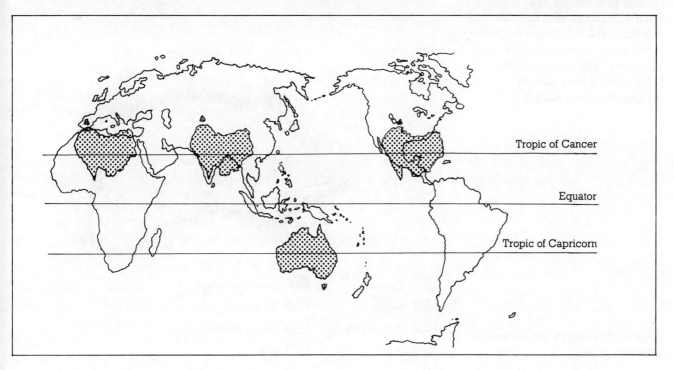

Tropic of Cancer

Equator

Tropic of Capricorn

Australia's annual rainfall pattern provides an indication of the areas receiving greatest rainfall. It should always be considered in conjunction with rates of evaporation, which are greatest in the driest parts of the continent.

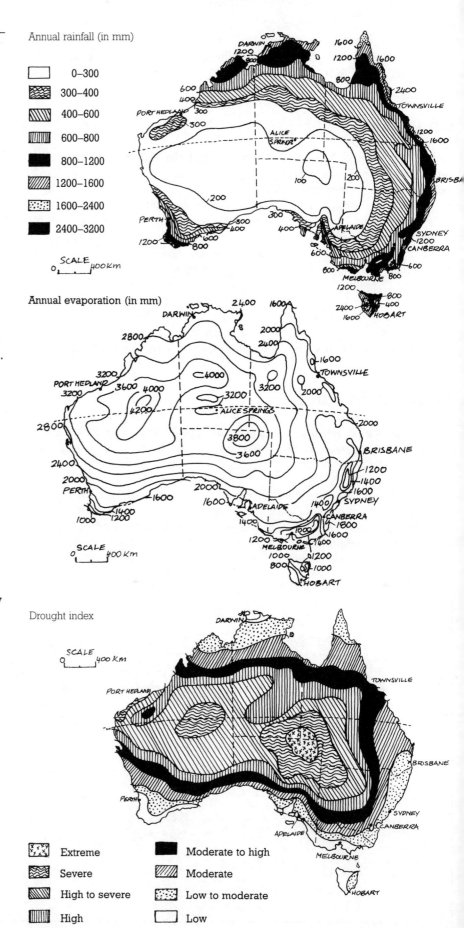

Annual rainfall

Sydney (1215 mm a year) receives almost exactly twice that of Melbourne (659 mm), both of which exceed London's rainfall (603 mm). The driest of Australia's capital cities is Adelaide (528 mm).

Annual evaporation rates

Some idea of the impact of evaporation on available water may be gained by comparing the annual evaporation rates for Australian cities with that for London (about 512 mm) — Sydney 1961 mm, Melbourne 1534 mm, Adelaide 1876 mm, and Perth 1977 mm, all have greater evaporation than rainfall.

(Maps courtesy of the Bureau of Meteorology)

Annual rainfall (in mm)

	0–300
	300–400
	400–600
	600–800
	800–1200
	1200–1600
	1600–2400
	2400–3200

Annual evaporation (in mm)

Drought index

Extreme		Moderate to high	
Severe		Moderate	
High to severe		Low to moderate	
High		Low	

or inland deserts of that State. Likewise *Caltha introloba*, from Australia's alpine areas, is not likely to do well in dry plains. In part, this relates to plant provenance (see pp. 27–8). Many of the plants available to us from Mediterranean climates have been collected from cool areas (e.g. *Genista aetnensis* (Mt Etna Broom) from the slopes of Mt Etna, in Sicily) rather than from hot, dry plains; many came to Australia via English nurseries.

When designing and planning your garden, note the effects that modify the area where your garden is. North and west slopes receiving more solar energy than south- and east-facing ones are therefore warmer, and may be more moisture stressed. South-facing slopes are the most protected.

Slopes exposed to winds will be different again. If the slopes receive hot, dry winds, then the damage caused by desiccation will be much greater than on the opposite slopes that are protected. When slopes are exposed to coastal winds, then damage from coastal salt may extend for a greater distance inland than where there are no slopes or the land is flat. Where slopes cause cloud to rise, the slopes facing the weather will be wetter than surrounding areas, while the opposite, protected slopes will receive less wind and will also be drier — a rain shadow. The choice of plants able to tolerate dry conditions becomes more important in this situation.

Consider temperature too. Increasing altitude means cooler conditions. However, in winter the coldest areas are in valleys; while the tops of mountains may be cold, the coldest, densest air flows down the hillside to collect in the valleys. The coldest (lowest) part of a garden can be protected by the use of dense plantings to shield and deflect cold air flow.

Micro-climates, as the name suggests, are small climatic areas relating to a specific site within a specific garden. The features are similar to those already mentioned, but are on a very small scale.

It is possible that there may be a rainshadow effect in the garden against the side of the house protected from the prevailing direction of rain. The wetter side may have a different set of plants from that of the dry side, which may need a separate watering system.

The north-facing wall of a house will be warmer than the south-facing one. Here full sun and reflected heat from the walls may reduce humidity and dry the soil, but the wall will also provide increased winter heat (vital in those situations where you may be trying to grow a plant that is not tolerant of our winter).

The shaded south side of a house, protected from direct sun, can be a good habitat for specific plants. You can influence this micro-climate with the shade of a pergola or vegetation.

Never ignore the effect of wind. Strong wind makes an area unpleasant to sit in, will dry out the garden and damage plants, especially for newly established gardens. Windbreaks are the solution. Use open structures (such as lattices) or plants.

Water for windbreaks

The plants you choose for windbreaks should be able to prosper in your current water regime, or you will find yourself adding water to keep them alive — a drip-irrigation system may be required to supply supplementary water. By reducing windspeeds a windbreak reduces evapotranspiration, water use by plants and water loss from the soil surface.

The effectiveness of a windbreak depends upon its height and its thickness. A large windbreak creates an enormous water demand.

Fenceline micro-climate

Fencelines also create micro-climates: the climate on the shaded side of a fence will be a little different from that on the exposed side. Any narrow strip between a house and a fence is likely to be consistently shaded, and probably damp — a very specific micro-climate.

Planning your garden for beauty and low water consumption

By understanding the requirements of your site, you can enjoy your garden and still reduce its water consumption. However, you must plan first.

Beauty is found in a diverse range of garden types and styles, sometimes depending upon your mood, but you must consider those principles that achieve the best results: scale or proportion, unity, space, style and texture.

How is the garden to work for you? For some of my friends it is an opportunity to rear chickens, grow a bit of bush, enjoy a spa and eat outside. Others prefer a tennis court and pool, but still have an eating area; for some it is a storage space for a car, a caravan, a boat and a plethora of other bits and pieces, as well as space for a barbecue and outdoor meal area. Spend some time discovering what a garden can do for you. Garden design has changed in the last decade, and people are moving away from the concept of a rectangle of paving, a square of lawn, a surrounding narrow planting bed, a Hills hoist and a pergola. How do you find about present trends?

Through Australia's Open Garden Scheme you can visit a large number of gardens throughout Australia. These vary from good to poor, and not all will meet your expectations. Even the most unlikely garden may offer something of interest to you — it may be the type of paving, or a particular association of plants. Ask questions, and note down the information you receive.

New housing estates often have demonstration gardens worth visiting, especially those established by government housing authorities — for example, the Urban Land Authority in Victoria is often at the forefront of implementing new low-water technologies. Demonstration water-efficient gardens have been built in many botanic gardens and in parks. Seek them out, and learn from them.

Many of your friends will have created a new garden or made over an existing one. Most people are willing to share their experiences with you, giving you advice about their mistakes and sharing information on their successes. This helps you to identify many of the pitfalls before you start.

Even if you don't read all the new books and magazines, look at the pictures, they can be most inspiring. They will also show the good and bad — and remember that the photographer may have known little about garden design. Books are generally better as a source of inspiration than magazines (see Further reading). Study any pictures and plans to understand why and how they work.

If you feel you cannot manage by yourself, you might perhaps employ a professional consultant. Check that landscape architects and garden designers understand and have sympathy for low-water gardens — many do not! Ask to see their work, and check out their fees. Though they may appear to be expensive, their work will add sufficient value to your property to cover their fees many times over. You will also save on your water rates! Design workshops at colleges, botanic gardens and other centres can be enormously helpful.

Identifying needs

Once you know what other people have done, get your own list together.

Most of you will want an outdoor eating area, located where it will be sunny at some parts of the day and shaded at others.

Recreational areas — a pool, a tennis court, a lawn, a child's playground — allow you to relax in your own garden. Plan them to suit your lifestyle.

In some respects your garden is really an extension of your home. As in the house, you will also have service areas — places for a garden shed, rubbish and compost bins, even for your car. These are best tucked away so they don't intrude on your leisure and pleasure spaces.

Site planning

Deciding what you wish to have in your garden is only part of your problem. Organise these elements in such a way that there is a logic about them, not only in terms of the part of the site they occupy but also in their relationship to each other. Consider the qualities of your site in terms of micro-climates when you plan: for example, your pool needs to be in plenty of sun, your vegetable garden too, your tennis court should preferably run north–south, while your barbecuing spot may be best if lightly shaded.

Part of this planning may be the use of vegetation to separate spaces: for example, a low lavender hedge, or trees to create shade. Create shade and windbreaks to reduce reflected heat and light that may make your garden uncomfortable. Draw a plan of your site.

Refer to the three designs in this book for further help in planning, or consult one of the recommended books in Further reading. However, these books are not likely to specifically consider the issue of making your garden water efficient. Now is the time for you to consider this.

The three plans show gardens of quite different sizes. They suggest strategies for different block sizes: clearly solutions that would suit a unit in an inner-city suburb may not be appropriate for a large rural property. Consider the full implications of lot size on the way you can design to save water, as well as the way the garden is to be used.

1 A small, inner-city or suburban garden

Urban consolidation is becoming more common, with large family homes demolished to make way for a cluster of smaller homes. These blocks are quite small, without room for many of the generous spaces of traditional gardens. Organisation is the key to using every space effectively.

Demonstration water-efficient gardens

These already exist in Darwin, Canberra and Melbourne, and more will be created. The information they give you will often explain water-efficient gardening in your area; this may include lists of plants especially suited to your area.

Measuring the site

With a friend, measure up the site, and plot it on graph paper so that 1 cm on your plan represents 1 metre on the ground. Lay transparent paper over the graph paper, and draw your ideas on this sheet.

Zone 1

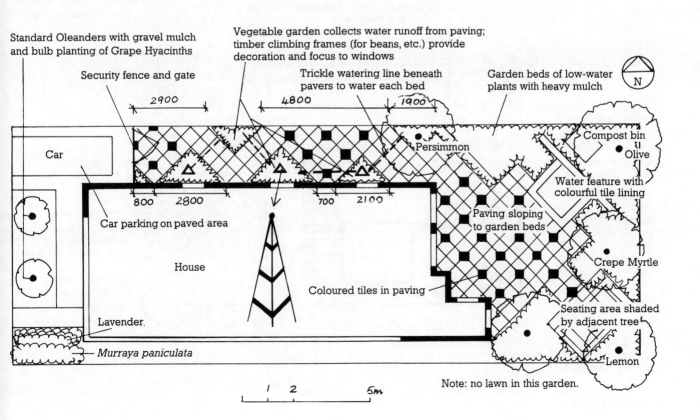

Standard Oleanders with gravel mulch and bulb planting of Grape Hyacinths

Security fence and gate

Vegetable garden collects water runoff from paving; timber climbing frames (for beans, etc.) provide decoration and focus to windows

Trickle watering line beneath pavers to water each bed

Garden beds of low-water plants with heavy mulch

2900

4800

1900

N

Car

Persimmon

Compost bin

Olive

800   2800

700   2100

Water feature with colourful tile lining

Car parking on paved area

Paving sloping to garden beds

House

Crepe Myrtle

Coloured tiles in paving

Lavender,

Seating area shaded by adjacent tree

Murraya paniculata

Lemon

1   2   5m

Note: no lawn in this garden.

Circular lawns

Circular lawns are the most sensible since these can be irrigated by a single pop-up sprinkler. Dish the area to hold water rather than letting it run off; the dishing should be very slight and not too obvious.

Add colour

Because of the restricted size of your garden, seek every opportunity to add a bit of colour to your garden. Use some coloured glazed tiles in your paving, and put plants in tubs. These tubs could be colourful glazed pots, chosen to relate to the colour of the tiles, or the waterwell type of pot that holds water in the reservoir.

Zone 2

- Grass is the single greatest user of water in our gardens; by doing away with it we will save not only considerable amounts of water but also the labour of mowing. You won't need a mower, and that is a saving too.
- Where space permits, you may wish to have a lawn, but design it to ensure efficient watering.
- Traditional small Islamic gardens used paving very effectively. By creating patterns they were both colourful and interesting. If paving is sloped towards the garden beds, rainfall is captured on the site.
- Lush vegetation in a small garden reduces the reflection of light and heat from walls and surfaces, and keeps your house cooler throughout summer. Deciduous trees give you winter light.
- You will be able to keep a small garden free of weeds very easily. Your home-made compost may provide sufficient mulch for the whole garden; if you grow plants profusely there will be little open soil.
- Choose plants wisely from among the lists throughout the book, especially on pages 57–61, to ensure they are tolerant of dry conditions, and locate them in places that best suit their requirements.

2 A typical 'quarter-acre' block

Of course, there is no such thing as a 'typical' block, no matter what its dimensions, for every garden is different, depending upon slope, soil, exposure, altitude, and so on. Yet the typical 'quarter-acre' block creates an image for Australians, so used have we become to this size of block.

This sized block permits far more activity than is possible in a courtyard garden, but inevitably there are also more places needing water. Zone water use; without some control you could be wasting water.

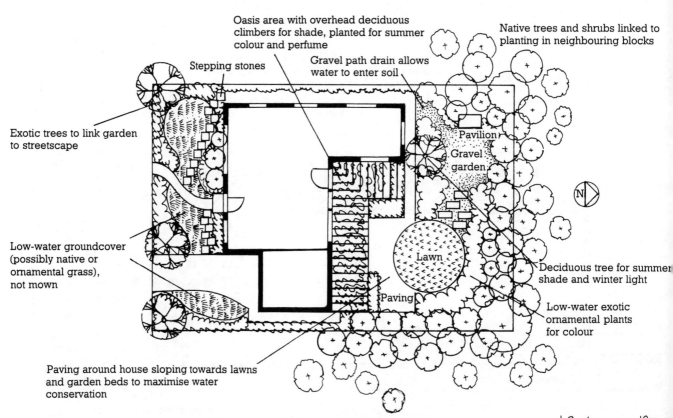

Oasis area with overhead deciduous climbers for shade, planted for summer colour and perfume

Native trees and shrubs linked to planting in neighbouring blocks

Stepping stones

Gravel path drain allows water to enter soil

Exotic trees to link garden to streetscape

Pavilion

Gravel garden

Low-water groundcover (possibly native or ornamental grass), not mown

Lawn

Deciduous tree for summer shade and winter light

Paving

Low-water exotic ornamental plants for colour

Paving around house sloping towards lawns and garden beds to maximise water conservation

1 2 4   10m

Just as was the case in the courtyard garden, by keeping the house cool in the summer, by shading it and creating a cooled micro-climate, you markedly reduce energy consumption. Establish oasis zones to the north and west of the house. Use plants to create shade. Pave these areas for outdoor eating. By relating these areas to the family room, the house effectively spills into the garden. The value of this luxuriant oasis retreat for any family from the heat of the summer sun is inestimable.

Beyond this, the garden can be less luxuriant, and should reflect more of your natural environment. I believe that garden design should become less formal as you move further from the house, into a less formal dryland garden.

Collect water from paved areas and lead it into the garden. Downpipes may assist in this, but on clay soils this may supply too much water that will drain slowly, and the cold, wet soil may slow growth. Plants gaining the benefit of such water may need little supplementary watering. Further away from the house there will be little water from the paving and little run-off, so this area will always be quite dry. Adding supplementary watering may be possible, but may not be necessary at all since in this zone you could grow drought-tolerant plants capable of growing without any additional water. This may not be necessary at all, however, since in this zone you could grow plants capable of surviving without any additional water.

Between the house and this driest part of the garden, you may choose to have a grass area. Grasses are soft and cool, and ideal for children's play. Part of the larger garden may need some additional water. Again, a circular lawn would be sensible. Shape this lawn so that any excess water runs to the driest part of the garden. Grass in this area should receive very limited supplementary water, just sufficient to keep it alive but not enough to encourage any lushness. Winter rain and growth will ensure this, but by summer's end this area may well be dry.

Selecting suitable low-water plants is vital, though you should consider putting plants with medium drought tolerance next to the house and the real toughies further away. I especially like the idea of using indigenous plants to attract wildlife. If your neighbours adopted this policy of indigenous planting it would create a network for wildlife movement through the suburbs.

Ask yourself why good gardens are good

Do they work in terms of allowing people to use them?

Is there sufficient space to sit or to eat outside?

Do they have places away from the searing intensity of the summer's sun?

Note the faults of gardens, you can learn much from them.

Since you are trying to create a garden that is not only beautiful but also water efficient, ask yourself how water efficient is the garden you are looking at.

Do you like the appearance and colours of the mulch?

Does it cover the soil effectively?

What are the most attractive plants?

Do they use water effectively?

3 The rural subdivision

I have never understood why rural shires insist on 4–10 hectare subdivisions. There are good reasons for allowing cluster housing, with extensive areas of open country being left as agricultural land or good bush.

The great temptation for the rural home-owner is to convert 2 or 3 hectares of this land into a garden, even if it is only grass that has to be regularly mown. What would be better is to have a smaller, more detailed and better-maintained garden close to the house and more extensive native planting beyond.

In this example the site is divided into three distinct areas, with that closest to the house maintaining the oasis concept — a shaded, irrigated and manicured extension to the house.

The second area is a midway step to the broader third area. This second area will have some watering, but only in extreme circumstances. Much of the water for this area is collected from paving and downpipes, and this provides adequate water for much of the year. Other water collected here is led directly to a dam in the third area, where water can be stored until it is pumped out as an adjunct to the water from tanks and the town supply.

Detailed planting in this second area will offer excellent colour and texture, blending native and exotic plants for their visual quality rather than for their

Preparations

Establishing vegetation can be expensive.

Use herbicides to control weed growth, rip the ground to ensure better root development, use direct seeding of seed of local provenance where possible, exclude grazing pests (e.g. rabbits), or farm stock from among the seedlings, and use mulch during the early years to secure growth.

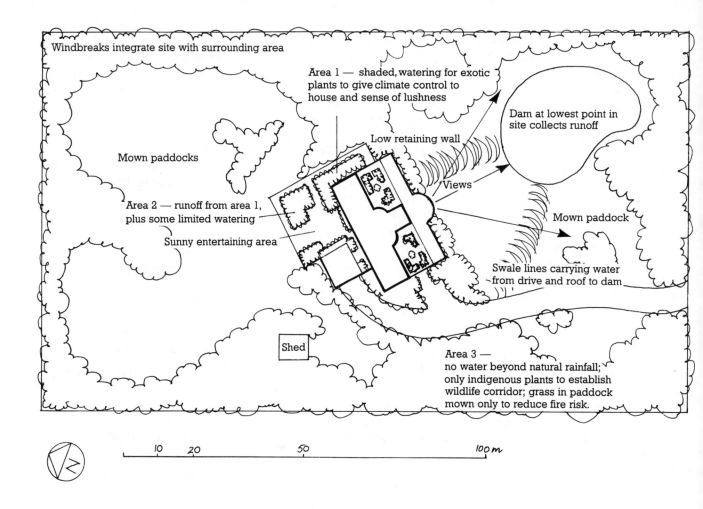

Windbreaks integrate site with surrounding area

Area 1 — shaded, watering for exotic plants to give climate control to house and sense of lushness

Dam at lowest point in site collects runoff

Low retaining wall

Mown paddocks

Views

Area 2 — runoff from area 1, plus some limited watering

Mown paddock

Sunny entertaining area

Swale lines carrying water from drive and roof to dam

Shed

Area 3 — no water beyond natural rainfall; only indigenous plants to establish wildlife corridor; grass in paddock mown only to reduce fire risk.

10   20   50   100 m

Zone 3

Drought-resistant hedge plants (up to 3m)

Drought tolerance: *** (high)
                    **, * (good)

Abelia × grandiflora	**
Callistemom viminalis 'Captain Cook'	**
Chaenomeles speciosa	*
Elaeagnus pungens	**
Eriostemon myoporoides	*
Escallonia macrantha	**
Hakea salicifolia	**
Leptospermum scoparium var. *rotundifolium*	*
Melaleuca incana	**
Pyracantha coccinea	**
Raphiolepis indica	***
Westringia fruticosa	**

country of origin. Larger blocks are well suited to the use of indigenous plants. Frequently they are sufficiently large to sustain populations of native birds and, providing dogs and cats are controlled and fences are not too restrictive, native animals. This will certainly be more feasible as the vegetation grows. Extensive areas of the garden should be of native trees and shrubs established from seed, both in the ground and collected from local trees.

Grass here should not be irrigated. While there may be growth in summers of high rainfall, in many years it will need no cutting as it dries out. However, long dry grass presents a major problem because of the risk of grass fire. Timing mowing is all-important here.

Massed indigenous vegetation gives a most dramatic effect, far more acceptable than those rows of golden cypress so frequently seen. Restrict exotics to areas close to the house, except perhaps where avenues lead along a driveway.

Design principles

You now have an idea of how gardens might be designed to reduce water consumption. Combine this with the irrigation principles, use of mulches, amelioration of soils, and so on, in this book. Also apply the traditional design principles below.

Unity

Don't use every garden feature and technique on one site. You will achieve more by keeping your design simple and bold, linking house and garden in style and mood. By selecting plants that tolerate dry conditions you will gain a unity of plant shape, foliage colour and character.

Style

All styles of gardens can be modified to be water efficient.

Formal gardens are symmetrical, and have more precise paving and plant groupings. Informal gardens are generally less structured, but they too need a visual balance.

Cottage gardens have been popular for the last few years and many of the plants grown in these gardens (lavenders, rock roses, roses, sages, and the like) have a low water demand. In the USA James van Sweden and Wolfgang Oehme use these plants in bold masses. Plant form must be especially striking here to hold interest.

Informal Australian plant gardens suit a particular style of house, perhaps one where mud brick has been used, while really formal gardens of clipped box, roses, and the like, suit more formal houses. To be really effective, planting, paving ornaments and furniture should all combine to achieve a particular overall style and effect.

Scale

All elements of the design, including the garden setting and the house, should be to the same scale. Too frequently gardens are designed with, say, small plants or narrow garden beds that do not relate to the scale of the external landscape: the scale of your landscape is governed by the sky, the horizon and the ground.

With fences and trees, shrub massings, and so on, you can change the scale of the garden to create spaces intimate in their scale (e.g. a seat beneath a tree) or more exposed and exciting (e.g. a view over distant countryside). If you refer to the zones in the third example, you can see that zone 1 represents the most intimate space, whereas zone 3 is generally more exposed, though spaces of an intimate scale could be established.

The scale of features created in the outdoor landscape are generally too small: paths are often too narrow, patios too small, planting beds too narrow and sometimes containing narrow ribbons of bedding plants.

Be bold. Plant in bold sweeps, create large and effective paved areas, be generous in landscape design.

Space

The building blocks of gardens are the spaces. Spaces are defined by changing materials horizontally (paving giving way to grass), vertically (a low hedge or a fence), and overhead (a pergola). Design spaces suitable for the particular functions, and then link them (by use of viewlines, axes, and so on) to create a logic for your site plan.

Garden features

You may be planning to include some of the following features in your garden design.

Decking

- This protects slopes near your house from erosion.
- It replaces lawn with its high water demand, and gives you a level surface for entertaining.

Drought-tolerant succulents

Drought tolerance: *** (high)
                      **, * (good)

Aeonium arboreum	***
A. 'Pseudotabulaeforme'	***
Agave attenuata	***
Aloe arborescens	***
A. striata hybrids	***
Carpobrotus hybrids	**
Crassula argentea	*
Echeveria imbricata	**
Lampranthus species	*
Senecio mandraliscae	**

Drought-resistant windbreak plants

Drought tolerance: *** (high)
                      **, * (good)

Acacia cyclops	***
A. dealbata	**
A. decurrens	*
A. longifolia	**
A. melanoxylon	*
A. retinodes	***
A. saligna	*
Allocasuarina torulosa	**
Callistemom citrinus	**
C. rigidus	**
C. viminalis	**
Cupressus macrocarpa	**
Eucalyptus erythrocorys	***
E. leucoxylon	***
Leptospermum laevigatum	**
Melaleuca armillaris	**
M. linariifolia	**
Myoporum laetum	*
Rhamnus alaternus	*
Westringia fruticosa	**

Pergolas and arbours create shade.

A pond or fountain

A small pond will inevitably require some water; but with a fine-spray fountain in a sheltered formal pond this water demand will be small. The beautiful sound of a delicate fountain refreshes and cools. (This device was used in the past in many of the great Islamic gardens, in spite of the scarcity of water.) To reduce evaporation, place your pond so that it is protected from direct sun and from wind.

- Where people walk barefoot (e.g. around a swimming-pool) the surface will remain cool.
- The addition of climbing plants on a lattice, will help to protect you from wind and sun.
- You will have a useful storage area below the decking.

Pergola or pavilion

- This will connect your house and garden spaces.
- If covered with climbing plants a pergola will give you shade in summer, and light in winter if you use deciduous plants.

Pond*

- This can be designed to hold rainwater run-off from roofs or paving.
- Reduce evaporation by growing shade and pond plants; and check there are no leaks.
- Suitably planted around the edges, your pond could become a popular part of a local wildlife corridor.

Swimming-pool*

- Use a pool cover to minimise evaporation.
- Remember that water emptied from your swimming-pool is chlorinated or saline, and therefore unsuitable for use on your garden.

Sundial, sculpture, bird bath, or arbour

- Ensure that you provide suitable spaces to view these features, and a contrast in surface textures in your plant groupings.

*Take appropriate precautions to protect children from accidents in or near water, and observe all legal requirements (fences, locked gate).

Ellis Stones created a small feature pond in this garden for a refreshing view without a great demand for water.

At Tipperary Church (York, WA), one of Australia's most successful private gardens, the use of grass is restricted, while paving provides a low-water surface and drought-tolerant plants ground-level interest. The eucalypts are a strong link between the artificial garden and the broader landscape. (PHOTO: LORNA ROSE)

ABOVE LEFT: Historically, large amounts of water were not available to gardeners, yet gardens were not uninteresting. Foliage and colour abounded, as may be seen in the Moonta (SA) Miner's Cottage garden, where a typical nineteenth-century garden has been reconstructed. (PHOTO: JOHN PATRICK)

ABOVE: *Cistus ladanifer*, a prolific-flowering Mediterranean shrub always looks fresh and attractive, and enjoys a sunny position. (PHOTO: JOHN PATRICK)

LEFT: Cacti and succulents are well suited to dry conditions. Careful combination of their forms and textures with the textures of rocks gives a wonderful picture, though the area is not really conducive to children's play and is an extremely hazardous area to bend in and weed. (PHOTO: JOHN PATRICK)

BELOW LEFT: Extravagant orange and yellow flowers make *Gladiolus natalensis* an eye-catcher in any garden. (PHOTO: JOHN PATRICK)

Soils and water

Soil is the single most important aspect of our gardens. Its quality varies from place to place because soil is a mixture of several components that vary in their proportions and character, depending on their origins. As well, the proportions of some of the components vary at different times, significantly affecting plant growth.

All gardeners would love to have a loamy soil with a combination of good waterholding and aeration, good nutrient availability and easy workability, but the fact is that most of us have a soil that has been modified, perhaps by the gardening habits of a previous owner, perhaps by a developer who has removed good soil from the site, or maybe by a careless builder or contractor with little concern for the wellbeing of the soil.

The soil profile is made up of different levels of soil. The top 600 mm or so is the most important, because it is here that oxygen is available to the roots, water enters the soil as rainfall or irrigation water, and fertilisers are applied either as leaf-fall or by our fertilising practices. Here, too, the activity of the soil micro-organisms is at its greatest, with a positive effect on soil quality.

Good top-soil is vital for your successful cultivation of plants:
- It serves as the anchorage place for the plant — but only if successful root penetration can be achieved, so soils must permit exploration by roots to achieve a sufficiently extensive spread to obtain stability.
- It provides the source of oxygen and water — the soil must permit their access to the soil.
- It is the source of nutrients — it should be sufficiently fertile to provide the required nutrients.

If your soil is to provide these benefits you should appreciate its qualities, and really get to know the soil on your block.

Analysing your soil

Soils are a combination of mineral particles, air, water, organic debris and living organisms. The proportions change from soil to soil, and the materials themselves may change. Consider soils before and after rainfall. Before rain the soil may be quite dry, with a large number of open pores filled with air. As rain falls the water is drawn into these pores, and the volume of air is reduced. Continued rainfall without effective drainage may lead the soil to become waterlogged, and eventually flooded. The volume of air in the soil will remain low as the soil remains waterlogged. This has an adverse effect on plant growth. Optimum growth is achieved when there is a correct balance of all of these

Composition of soil

Assess the composition of your soil by placing a small handful in a beaker, cover this with water, and shake the beaker.

Allow the soil to settle, and observe how it settles out in a series of layers, each grading into the next.

The largest particles settle out first to give a basal layer and lighter, smaller particles settle progressively more slowly until the water is almost clear. Note that you will also have some organic detritus floating on the surface.

The proportions of different components will vary markedly.

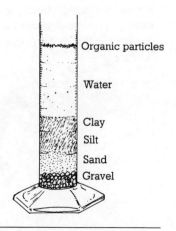

Organic particles

Water

Clay
Silt
Sand
Gravel

Soil and water shaken in a container will settle out, with coarsest soil at the base and finest on the top; organic particles float on the surface.

Testing soil texture

To assess the overall quality of your soil do a simple hand-test.

1 Take a small handful of your soil and wet it slowly. (Add just enough water so that the soil does not stick to your fingers but is moist enough to glisten to the eye.)

2 Work the soil with the palm and fingers of one hand to form a ball of soil, or bolus, that is evenly mixed with no lumps remaining.

3 Try pushing out a ribbon of soil between your forefinger and thumb. Use the following guide to assess your soil type by its texture.

soil qualities: balanced water and soil oxygen, fertiliser availability, and so on. By understanding your soil you will learn what changes you can make to bring the soil to the 'ideal'.

Look at the texture of your soil. The mineral content of your soil has built up as a result of the weathering of minerals over hundreds of thousands of years by many weathering agents: water, wind, heat and cold, the action of glaciers and plant roots, even the action of lichens on rock surfaces. Different types of rocks erode at different speeds: sandstone graves in a cemetery are more eroded than marble graves of a similar age, bluestone steps on old houses have eroded by wear. This process is continual, albeit generally quite slow. This erosion leads to soil particles of quite different sizes. Look at your own soil: you will probably find some large pieces called gravels that can be picked out individually, as well as tiny particles, almost too small to see. Depending upon their size, soil particles are given different names: gravels, sands, silts and clays (see table). The quantities of these different particles in a soil will vary, as will the character of the soil as the proportions of particles change. This may not be an entirely natural process — it could result from the work of builders who may have left mortar in your soil or piled up sand in one part of the garden, resulting in an increase in the proportion of larger particles.

Soil quality depends not only on the texture but also on the structure of the soil — the way the soil is held together with pore spaces, organic materials and different-sized soil particles. This structure is vital, and may be lost when wet soil is worked or cars and equipment parked on it, leading to loss of soil fertility.

Soil texture guide

Texture	Ribbon length	Comments
Sand	No ribbon can be made	Gritty, coarse or fine sand, cannot be moulded
Loamy or clayey sand	0–0.5cm	Slight coherence, gritty
Sandy loam	1.5–2.5cm	Coherent but gritty
Loam	2.5–3.5cm	Smooth and coherent, but not gritty. May be spongy if high in organic matter
Clay loam	3.5–5.0cm	Feels plastic and smooth. Some fine sand may be present
Clays	5.0cm or longer	Like plasticine; some sand may be present

The result will depend upon the nature of the soil: clay soils will stick together, larger sand particles will not bind.

Water

Water is critical for plant growth, and the better the rainfall is absorbed into the soil, the more will be available for plants. Soil is like a great reservoir, and depending upon the soil's structure different quantities of water are held and available to plants.

Plants may wilt towards the end of the day. During the night, however, when transpiration rates are low, the plants are able to regain turgidity. Without further rainfall or irrigation the plants will again wilt, but may regain turgidity. However, the stage will be reached when there is not sufficient water for plants to regain their form — either the water is too remote, or the energy required to obtain it is too great. The plants have now reached permanent wilting point:

the difference between field capacity and permanent wilting point is the available water.

When a plant reaches permanent wilting point it does not mean that there is no further water in the soil. There is, but it is so strongly held by the surface tension of the soil that it takes enormous energy by the plant to obtain it. At permanent wilting point there is considerably more water in clays than in sands.

Water penetration into soils is vitally important. If water does not penetrate, then it does not become available to plants. Compacted soil layers are one impediment to water movement, but so, too, are sand layers in clay. By contrast, water will move down a sand column. In maintaining grass areas sand is added to compacted soil in columns.

Air

Air is critically important in soil, not because of its effect on water consumption but because the growth of roots requires air to be present. Equally importantly, the presence of oxygen in the air is essential for the survival of soil organisms vital for the wellbeing of the soil. Water and air can pass quickly into soil through the tunnels made in the soil by worms and other organisms.

Organic matter

Organic matter is a vital element in soil, but sometimes is absent, especially from purchased soils. Organic material is essential for improving all soils as it provides the food for worms, with their attendant benefits. Organic materials break up the structure of clays and provide sandy soils with a means of holding water and nutrients. Their presence is essential for a healthy soil, and contributes to a good soil structure.

Improve soils for plant growth and water efficiency

Improve your soil for more efficient use of water.

Clay soils and sandy soils have different problems: clay soils can be compacted, but the size of the particles in sandy soils is such that these sandy soils retain reasonable drainage and aeration. Sandy soils leach quickly (nutrients are lost because water moves rapidly through the soil) but it is possible to grow plants on sandy soils with short but frequent watering. Fertilisers are moved quickly from the soil. Slow-release fertilisers are a little more expensive, but their rate of nutrient release suits sandy soils very well.

In extreme conditions improve your sandy soil by adding both clay and organic material to bring the structure closer to a loam. There is a limit to the volume of clay that is practicable to cultivate into a sandy soil; usually restricted to the top 15–20 cm. Add clay, equivalent to one-quarter of the volume of sand being treated, to the sand, together with large quantities of organic material (say, 10 cm of compost). Top this up with ongoing applications of organic mulch to enhance the worms' food source.

Sometimes sandy soils repel water, as the result of the particles being coated with waxes produced by fungi. Water may sit for some time on the soil surface as pools, without moving through the sand. The use of clays, as described above, will aid in wetting the soil; alternatively, use a wetting agent.

Water-absorbing granules assist water storage in sandy soils. They hold many times their weight of water, which is then available to plants, reducing the need for watering at a critical time, or in establishing a planting. The granules have a life of a few months, which may be sufficient to get plants through their first vital season of growth.

Modification of clay soils is more likely to be necessary if they have been compacted. Just as clay can be added to sand to improve its structure, so too

Soil water

Water bonded in the actual soil structure cannot be obtained by any plant. More water is then absorbed in the surface of the soil by surface tension. You can see this when you place a small amount of soil on a drop of water. The water is drawn into the soil, and held there by surface tension.

Particle size

A sand particle has a certain surface area on to which water can be absorbed, but clay particles of the same volume have a far greater surface area for water absorption. This water may be available, but it requires enormous energy by the plant to remove it, and so most remains unavailable. Following rainfall, however, water moves down into the soil through the force of gravity. Its speed of movement depends upon the type of soil involved. Where the soil is very sandy, there are continuous pore spaces, through which the water can move very quickly.

In clay

Clay soils, however, may have more overall pore space, but there is little connection of these pores. Where the clay is really heavy the movement of water is very slow.

Field capacity

When water fills these spaces, the soil is said to be at field capacity. This water is available to plants, and is easily removed from the soil by the root hairs.

Water moves deeper into sandy soil and generally roots penetrate these soils more deeply, not only to seek the water but also because of the oxygen gradient. In clay soils, however, the movement of water is relatively slow, and may pond on the soil surface before penetrating the pore spaces. Plants use this available water, but as the soil becomes drier the water is less easily available.

Sand column helps water penetration and
aeration of grass roots.

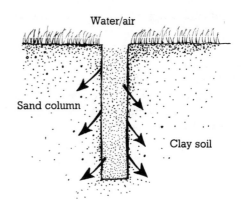

Water/air

Sand column

Clay soil

Wetting agents

Wetting agents need to be diluted
according to the supplier's
instructions, and applied slowly
enough to the soil to soak deeply
into the sand. Help the process
along by using a fork to create
holes through the sand and ensure
deeper wetting. These wetting
agents are effectively long-lasting
detergents, which break down the
waxy surface to ensure good water
take-up. They remain active for
some time, and are available from
most nurseries.

sand may be added to clay. However, if only small amounts of sand are added,
the sand becomes lost in the vast volume of clay. If sufficient sand is to be
added to the clay to have an overall effect, the volume of sand would have to
be very large. It is preferable to add sand where it will give the greatest benefit,
where drainage is most essential (e.g. where citrus trees or vegetables are to
be grown). Many trees and shrubs will grow well in clay soils containing both
nutrients and water. Clay soils can be improved relatively inexpensively.

Any compacted layers should be shattered, by ripping if possible, to encourage water and oxygen movement and deeper root penetration. Adding gypsum
may help, but it doesn't work on every soil. Test to see whether your soil will
respond to the application of gypsum. If the test result is positive, apply gypsum
to your soil at a rate between 0.5 and 1 kg per square metre. The benefits of
gypsum will remain for as long as there is gypsum in the soil; an ongoing, say
annual, addition of gypsum will be beneficial.

The other improvement for clay soils is to incorporate organic matter. This
is in some ways a universal panacea for clay and sandy soils; both benefit from
its addition. Most importantly, organic material establishes routes for oxygen
and water movement through the soil, and encourages worm activity. Organic
mulches will release nutrients and generally improve the soil's structure and its
water-holding capacity.

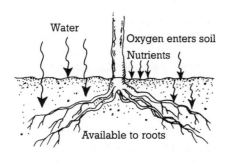

Water

Oxygen enters soil

Nutrients

Available to roots

Roots generally occupy upper soil levels.

Plants in containers and hanging baskets

Inevitably, plants in containers and hanging baskets need careful watering
because they do not have access to the surrounding soil to seek more water.
The mixes in these containers generally have good pore spaces and, as a result,
tend to dry out quickly, so watering is important.

As they are above ground-level these plant containers also get hot. Raised
baskets may have the cooling benefit of some air movement, but this is likely
to dry the container by evaporation. Only baskets with coconut fibre or similar
liners will benefit. The roots of plants in plastic pots may be killed.

Similarly, terracotta pots are cooled by evaporation. This evaporation does
not occur in plastic or glazed containers. Unglazed pots need more frequent
watering to compensate for the resulting water loss. Root damage may occur
on the side of any plastic pots facing the sun.

Just as wilting provides evidence of water shortage among in-ground plants,
so too it does for those in containers. The open nature of most potting mixes
results in rapid water movement, and may lead to quite rapid drying. The
surface of a mix will dry quite quickly, but if the lower part of the growing
medium is moist watering can wait. Many pots exposed to the sun will be
subject to surface evaporation, and a surface mulch will reduce water loss.

Containers

The watering requirements of
small containers can be assessed
by lifting them to feel their weight:
light containers need watering.
Knock the side of a large container;
if it sounds hollow it may need water.

The water-well types of pots are
very useful in this context because
the well gives a clear picture of
when water is required, and the
well can simply be topped up until
full. Trials have shown that these
containers provide a major saving
in water consumption, compared
with the usual luxury watering
given by most home gardeners.

How plants survive with less water

Dracaena draco (Dragon Tree) is an extraordinary plant from the Canary Islands. It is close to extinction in the wild, but provides a visually exciting low-water element for any landscape.

Given the opportunity to fly over the Earth's surface you would be able to note changes in the vegetation cover. The contrast between different vegetation zones would be very marked. In any as-yet-unfelled tropical rainforest, enormous trees and vines provide a lush green forest cover that uses the available rainfall to create the most biologically diverse habitats on Earth.

Elsewhere, and in complete contrast, desert environments may be so extreme that they contain no plants at all; they may have no available water and such extreme conditions of cold that no plants grow. If any rain does fall, then seeds lying dormant in the desert sands may produce a fleeting display of colour. After fleeting rainfall *Boerhaania repens* (an annual plant growing in the Sahara Desert) germinates, grows, flowers and produces seed in 10–14 days.

The cold environments of our alpine areas are different. Blanketed by a layer of winter snow, plants may be insulated from the worst of the cold conditions. As the snows melt they enjoy plentiful moisture, and quickly come into flower to enjoy the relatively short growing season. However, these areas may become exceptionally dry in the summer as they are exposed to full sun, and plants may be growing on a quickly draining scree. In mid-summer these may be extremely dry environments, while during cold weather any water may be frozen. What would be noticeable is that similar climatic zones throughout the world are dressed with parallel vegetation. In other words, alpine plants the world over have similar adaptations to their environment, as do rainforests.

The same is true for drylands. Whether you were to look down upon the dry landscapes of Europe (in the Mediterranean basin), or of California, the Middle East, South America, South Africa or south-western Australia, you would see that in spite of their geographical separation, they are remarkably consistent in their vegetation. These areas have 400–500 mm of rainfall, and scrub is the dominant vegetation type, forming a dense thicket.

In those areas where rainfall is a little higher, or where the water is drained and may collect for much of the year, there may be trees lining the creeks. Pomegranates, poplars, mulberries,. walnuts and planes grow naturally in this habitat in the Middle East.

These larger trees require more water than scrub environments receive, but where rainfall is a little higher the scrub gives way to a landscape of open savannah with trees and grassland. This vegetation type once covered extensive areas of south-eastern Australia, and may still be seen in many grassland areas; for example, *Eucalyptus melliodora* (Yellow Box) and *E. leucoxylon* (Yellow Gum) often remain as remnants in land that is now largely cleared.

Where conditions become drier (below 250 mm, for example) shrubs become more widely spaced to reduce competition. Eventually these give way

Plants with grey leaves

Some plants from the Mediterranean area have grey leaf colouration (e.g. the widely grown *Argyanthemum haouarytheum* from the Canary Islands, and *A. frutescens*, deservedly popular in Australia, with a very good tolerance of drought. *A. haouarytheum* is native to especially dry zones).

The best known Californian grey-foliaged plant is the lovely *Romneya coulteri* (Californian Tree Poppy), which produces large, pure white, tissue-like petals around a golden globe of stamens like the purest of free-range egg yellows. Penstemons are another of the groups of Californian plants with light-grey foliage.

The South African *Melianthus major* (Honey Flower) is a popular garden plant in Australia. It fits well into the grey garden theme, currently fashionable as an approach to garden design.

Drought resistance

Drought-resistant plants avoid the loss of water by evaporation through:

- light foliage colour
- thick, waxy cuticle or hard leaves
- stomata (openings in the leaf surface) deeply set in the leaves, frequently on the underside
- closing stomata during the day and only operating them at night when water loss is least
- leaves covered by scales or small, fine hair
- reduced size of leaves, in some cases to such an extent that they are no thicker than pine needles, as in cacti
- fewer leaves, and leaf loss in periods of stress.

Drought avoidance

Plants avoid drought by:

- a short life-cycle after rainfall, from germination and growth, to seeding
- a bulbous or rhizomatous rootstock, permitting survival through adverse conditions
- reducing competition by growing at remote distances from neighbouring plants
- developing an extensive root system to permit the plant to explore remote water sources
- developing ways to direct water to the root zone.

Agave attenuata (Foxtail Agave) is excellent in containers and as an accent plant for low-water gardens.

to succulents with a great capacity to store water from brief seasonal rainfall, or to produce a seasonal display.

My purpose in giving this brief account of habitats is threefold.

Firstly, Australians are not alone in experiencing low rainfall and high summer temperatures. By studying parallel environments and vegetation, we can establish which plants suited to our climate do not require large amounts of energy or water. The plant lists (pp. 57–62) mention some of the countries of origin of those plants suited to our environment.

Secondly, these habitats exist as ecosystems, and not as individual plants. These associations of plants reflect their environment, the soil, the solar energy, the temperature and, of course, the water that is available to them. We have already mentioned the broad changes in the vegetation make-up, depending upon changes in rainfall. Similarly your garden is a system, and the most effective and efficient use of water will be achieved by creating a garden of plants with similar demands for water.

Thirdly, and perhaps most significantly, these dryland associations reflect consistency in plant response to dry environments. Some are quite obvious and easily appreciated, others are less obvious and may be understood only upon closer inspection of plants. After studying these adaptations we know which water-efficient plants to select.

Plants growing in dry environments have two basic techniques for surviving dry conditions: drought resistance, and drought avoidance.

Light foliage colour

To reduce our own body temperature in the summer we wear light-coloured clothes, while houses in hot environments are often white to reflect heat. By contrast the darker clothing of winter warms us by absorbing heat.

Similar effects are achieved by plants developing paler foliage colour. Rainforest foliage is lush and dark green; in drier savannah grassland environments or the shrub habitats foliage colour changes to sage greens and greys. In many cases this is the result of the colour of the leaf hairs, in others the foliage colour derives from leaf pigments themselves. Lighter-coloured foliage remains cooler and has a lower water demand, losing less water from the surface. Many eucalypts have light-green or sage-green foliage. The beautiful *Eucalyptus caesia* (Gungurru), in addition to foliage colour, has vertically hanging leaves and a heavy white wax bloom over all branches, further water-conserving devices.

Grey leaves are common to all the dryland floras of the world.

Thick waxy cuticle or hard leaves

To understand how adaptations help suit plants to their environment by utilising less water, you need to understand how plants work. As you know, soils contain water, only some of which is available to plants. This available water is taken into the plant, mostly through the fine root hairs, so there are advantages in possessing an extensive root system. The water carries dissolved minerals through the plant.

Of the water drawn in through the roots of the plant 95–99 per cent passes through the plant and only 1–5 per cent is used.

In temperate parts of the world as much water passes into the atmosphere through the leaves of plants as enters the sea in rivers.

Anything that assists plants to reduce this water loss is beneficial, such as a thick or waxy cuticle (the outer surface of the leaf). While most water loss takes place through the stomata (the leaf surface openings), some is lost through the cuticle, especially by those plants with a thin cuticle.

It is not only a thickening of cell walls that reduces water loss but also the presence of a waxlike material, cutin, that helps water conservation. This has already been mentioned as occurring on the stems of *Eucalyptus caesia* (Gungurru), though, in general, little water loss takes place through plant stems.

This waxy layer may also cause leaves to become quite hard. This is easily seen with many of the pines, some of which have excellent drought tolerance.

The same plant may produce different types of leaves: sun leaves, and shade leaves. When exposed to the sun those leaves may develop a typical thick cuticle, while those in shaded areas are thinner (they do not have to reduce water loss like sun leaves do). This may have a significant effect on water consumption if, for example, a plant established in a shaded location is suddenly exposed to sun, or if a plant is pruned back and its sun foliage is removed to reveal only shade foliage, the physiological shock may be very marked.

Controlling water loss

The stomata are vital places for water loss on the plant for, as carbon dioxide is taken in, the plant may become susceptible to water loss.

The opening and closing of stomata is a complex procedure. When moisture is plentiful, the stomata open, but as water becomes less plentiful they close to prevent water loss. Stomata on the upper surface of a leaf will be fully exposed to the sun, so that evaporation will be high; they are also exposed to windflow, and both of these factors will increase water loss. Those on the underside of the leaf are protected and lose less water. Plants with most stomata on the lower side will be considerably better off.

Not surprisingly, plants with particularly effective drought tolerance have developed further ways to reduce water loss, most notably through sunken stomata. These are now no longer subject to wind-movement effects, furthermore they are insulated to some degree from direct sunlight.

Leaves with hairs and scales

In the creation of garden micro-climates the movement of wind across a garden can be controlled by the use of windbreak plantings.

Take this to a still smaller scale and imagine that, instead of being in a forest ourselves, an ant is among the hairs on the surface of a leaf. You may get some idea of the micro-climate effect achieved by leaf hairs. They offer a windbreak device to the surface of a leaf, and so reduce the rate at which evaporation takes place.

The layer of leaf hairs allows the humidity of the air immediately above the leaf surface to remain high (whereas wind movement on a smooth leaf would disperse this) and the plant no longer releases water into the atmosphere. Scales achieve a similar effect, reducing airflow over the leaf surface, and thus assisting in water conservation.

Leaf hairs maintain an insulating layer of air around a leaf in winter, while the light hair colour assists in maintaining lower summer temperatures.

Leaf hair is one of the most recognisable and useful indicators of drought

Water loss

Water loss through the cuticle in shaded environments may reach 10 per cent — ferns often have thin cuticles, and they may lose 30 per cent of transpired water through the cuticle. In their moist and shaded environment this matters little.

At the other extreme, desert plants have thick cuticles and lose no water through the cuticles. Visit any garden that contains cacti, and note the thickness of the leaf cuticles. Not only cacti reveal this adaptation, as you can see for yourself if you grow the delightful, drought-tolerant perennial *Sedum spectabile* (Ice Plant). Clearly, for plants attempting to conserve water, this 10 per cent is a very significant amount, and may make the difference between a plant's survival and its death.

Plants with hairs or scales

Few gardens do not possess at least one drought-tolerant plant with this adaptation, for example, *Lavandula dentata* (Lavender), *Salvia officinalis* (Sage), *Westringia fruticosa* (Coastal Rosemary) and *Leucophyta brownii* (Cushion Bush).

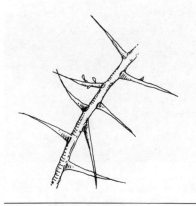

The reduced foliage of *Acacia acanthoclada* restricts water loss.

tolerance. The same leaf hairs may cause problems for plants in humid environments, where the moisture levels around leaves become high. Since the temperatures are also high, fungal activity can become significant. Many downy plants suffer extensively in humid areas (e.g. the ever-popular *Lavandula dentata* (French Lavender)).

Plants with spines

Cacti are special adaptations to very dry conditions and are never likely to be very popular for Australian low-water gardens, not least because of the image they create of dusty dryness, though many are superbly beautiful in flower. They have some interesting adaptations: some have a rippled margin, giving an increase in protection from water loss by achieving a further micro-climate modification. They are extreme examples of water conservation.

Small leaves

Plants with very large leaves will lose more water than those with small ones; they have a greater wind resistance, and thus are more prone to losing water than small leaves. However, small leaves may have more stomata per centimetre of leaf surface than large leaves, and move water quite rapidly only when water is plentiful. They can survive quite contentedly on a reduced regime.

Where leaf sizes of many of the most drought-tolerant trees are small or long and slender, wind resistance is minimised. Eucalypts are a prime example. Their leaves offer the least wind resistance, reducing their water loss, and help to control their temperature and reduce transpiration by offering the least surface to the sun. Eucalypts, however, have not taken the ultimate step of losing their leaves altogether.

Acacias frequently have a leaf-like structure (a phyllode), but some (e.g. *Acacia spinescens* (Spiny Wattle)) have neither leaves nor phyllodes. Not surprisingly, this species has excellent ability to tolerate drought.

Many people find the cacti, with their lack of foliage, unattractive, yet plants with reduced foliage are highly desirable in dry gardens.

A short life-cycle

One way of avoiding the stresses created by drought is to simply pack up when the going gets tough. Why hang around when you're likely to be fried to a crisp anyway?

Annual plants (those that complete their life-cycle from germination through flowering, pollination and seed production within a single year) are opportunistic, occupying spaces in the ecosystems that are frequently short term (for example, those spaces where light suddenly becomes available in a forest because a tree falls or areas where the existing cover is lost, say, through land slip).

Australian desert environments are dominated by annuals, which complete their life cycle within three months, only germinating when rainfall provides adequate moisture.

Annuals responding to rainfall occupy the most extreme environment. Where rainfall occurs annually in sufficient quantities to allow good plant growth, these annuals tend to grow in the season most favourable for light, temperature and water, producing seed before the dryness and heat of summer becomes apparent.

Dietes grandiflora (Wild Iris) has become increasingly popular in recent years because of its outstanding foliage, ongoing flowering display, and low water demands.

One of the characteristic features of dryland annuals is that their seeds remain viable for an extremely long time, and survive throughout droughts and from one wet period to the next.

Underground storage: bulbs, rhizomes, corms

Plants with this type of adaptation reveal similar characteristics to annual plants, but are perennial, and retain their vegetative parts until conditions are suitable for growth. They are unlikely to be as drought tolerant as annuals, but many are certainly well suited to southern Australia (from WA to NSW).

The clearly defined patterns of growth of bulbous plants allow them to survive the most adverse conditions of their environment, including extremes of winter cold as well as drought. Given the rainfall patterns of southern Australia, select bulbous plants with a tolerance of winter rainfall and summer drought, though it would be best to avoid those demanding winter chill before flowering, since in most southern areas the mild winters are insufficiently cold to initiate flowering. There are exceptions to this, and these are the areas where diverse collections of bulbs are frequently grown by enthusiasts (e.g. the Dandenongs, near Melbourne). This adaptation, of course, is vital in helping these species survive periods of intense cold, the plants only developing when the period of greatest cold is over.

An extensive range of bulbs is well suited to cultivation in our gardens, either without any supplementary water or with a limited amount of water when conditions become extreme.

Reduced competition for water

Where a resource is limited there is competition for that resource. This is certainly true where water is restricted. One way to reduce competition is by wider spacing of competing individuals or specimens.

In savannah woodland the dominant trees are generally widely spread in the open grassland so that they do not compete with each other. Similarly, as conditions get drier, desert shrubs grow as isolated specimens. Photographs of inland Australia and southern Mexico are both characterised by a dotty planting, the isolated plants being separated by areas of open soil.

In the home garden we want plants to relate in flower and textural associations. Supplementary watering helps to overcome this competitive problem and achieve good growth.

This spacing of plants due to competition is further complicated by the process of allelopathy (a chemical is released by one plant into the environment to inhibit the growth of other plants). This is not uncommon. Grasses, for example, restrict the production of fruit by apple trees by producing inhibiting chemicals. In dryland environments of southern California sage shrubs (*Salvia* sp.) appear to restrict the growth of grasses by the production of volatile oils with an inhibiting effect on grass growth.

Extensive root system

Roots are the point of entry of water into a plant. The development of an effective root system is vital to ensure adequate water provision for the survival of the plant. The root hairs absorb water, so it is essential that these hairs are able to explore for soil water. Of course, as soil water is utilised, new areas of

Plants without leaves

Many members of the pea family (Fabaceae) have lost their leaves or have reduced them to thorns (e.g. in the native *Daviesia brevifolia* (Leafless Bitter Pea)). This plant is native to well-drained gravels and sands, and has an intolerance of high water regimes. This adaptation, like so many others, is taken to extremes by cacti, which have lost leaves altogether, retaining only spines, and undertaking the entire photosynthesis process in their stems, where transpiration is also located.

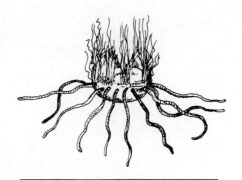

Eremurus bungei grows deeper in dry soils than in moist clays.

Root growth

A two-year-old specimen of a grass (*Agropyron cristatum*) was shown to have over 500km of roots, occupying a cylindrical soil volume 1.2 metres in diameter and 2 metres deep. Not all of this root system absorbs water at the same rate, the maximum amount being absorbed by root hairs, which of course permits an enormous area of contact between roots and the films around soil particles. Root hairs may increase the root surface area by over three thousand times, and thus enormously increase the volume of soil tapped. The *A. cristatum* must have produced almost 10km of root a week if growth rates were consistent, though this is unlikely.

So enormous do many root systems become as water is sought from distant parts of the soil that four-fifths of some plants from the Rub al-Khali desert in southern Arabia lie beneath the ground, while their roots may extend to a depth of 30 metres.

Some plants in this desert, where it may not rain for thirty years, are said to be drawing water today from ground deep below the desert that fell as rain more than 1000 years ago. Trees from desert areas, such as some species of tamarisks and mesquites, have been claimed to have roots up to 50 metres deep to plumb deeply stored water.

Festuca ovina glauca has a large fibrous root system to exploit deep water sources.

soil must be explored. Therefore, we can expect plants to have a rapid rate of root growth. Evidence suggests that this is indeed the case.

Tap-root structure is typical of young plants, which quickly develop it to ensure survival, seeking out water that may lie beneath the soil. However, as plants mature they begin to develop a more fibrous system, closer to the soil surface. Here the roots are able to obtain the benefit of even very restricted rainfall and dew, so characteristic of desert environments. However, these shallow roots may also be subjected to considerable heat, so mulching helps.

Similar effects may be seen with perennials. The small-leaved *Festuca ovina glauca* (Blue Grass) provides a huge fibrous root system, divided into fine roots that can penetrate an extraordinary volume of soil as well as very deep; just try digging an established specimen out of your garden.

Watering the root system

Some plants may be able to absorb water into their leaves (e.g. dew). These small volumes of water may make the difference between survival and death.

However, where plants have a waxy cuticle it is difficult for water to be absorbed. Waxiness is designed to prevent water loss, but it also has the disadvantage of preventing water entry! What can happen is that plants develop foliage with a V-shaped leaf cross-section. This effectively provides a valley structure, carrying water down the foliage to the base of the plant where it can enter the soil. While this may be only a very limited addition to the soil water, it can be quite significant in terms of plant survival (on the San Francisco Peninsula trees add up to 74 cm of water to the soil in this way; the normal annual precipitation in this area is only 64 cm a year).

Swollen trunks

Plants can store water within their structure, obtaining as much water as possible while it is available, and holding it for use when conditions become more stressful. Many cacti possess large cells within their walls, able to hold significant amounts of water. Because the cell walls are so thin they can lose water without damage. These cells are held within swollen stems and leaves.

Wilting

An obvious sign of water stress by plants on hot days is wilting: leaves change from being turgid to flaccid and hanging. This is a typical reaction for many plants minimising water loss (e.g. eucalypts), their pendulous leaves reduce their wind resistance and thus their water loss. Other plants without this adaptation will have problems. Wilting is a realistic response to water stress, and signifies an effort by the plant to reduce its use of water. Water in the soil may be in short supply, so that the plant has to use greater energy to obtain the water. This is most likely to become apparent in the afternoon; if a number of days go by with high temperatures and no rainfall, it may become apparent earlier in the day.

Wilting does not mean that there is no available water in the soil, though there will eventually be a point at which no more water is available to a plant, even though it is transpiring, and it is unable to obtain water from the soil.

In the evening, as the stomata close down, water loss through transpiration is reduced, and water absorption by roots is able to match, or indeed exceed, water loss. After a night of low water use, the leaves may again be turgid. This temporary wilting may continue for several days. It may have only a limited effect on the long-term wellbeing of the plant, but, if it continues for an extended period so that the plant cannot recover without further water, it reaches permanent wilting point. At this stage the plant will suffer.

Stunted growth may occur, with a reduction in flowering, low seed production, and ultimately the death of the plant. Wilting is easy to observe in some plants (e.g. hydrangeas), which produce flaccid leaves on hot days even when there is considerable water available; however, it is less easy to identify in plants with stiff foliage (e.g. camellias or rhododendrons).

Wilting does not necessarily imply that water is required, for the plants may well recover the next day. Too frequently gardeners see wilting plants and immediately turn to their watering systems or hoses to correct a perceived shortage. In fact, in the early stages at least, the plant is simply commenting on the heat of the day. Ongoing wilting does suggest that watering would be advisable.

Succulents

The most successful succulents are, of course, the cacti, which hold and draw upon large volumes of water held in their tissue. This also occurs in *Brachychiton rupestris* (Bottle Tree), which contains pithy fibrous material in the trunk, again allowing excellent water storage. Not surprisingly, these trees make outstanding specimens for low-water environments.

Choosing plants for the home garden

All these plant adaptations will affect the water economy of home gardens. Not all plants possess all of these adaptations, though many possess more than one.

Not all of these adaptations will be apparent when you inspect plants in your local nursery. Certainly grey foliage or hairy leaves will be obvious, bulbs and rhizomes too may be quite evident, but the presence of stomata on the underside of the leaves in sunken pits will not be very apparent!

For pointers on the best plants for your site when you buy plants from your local nursery, consult the lists of plants in the side columns, and the list of outstanding dry garden plants (pp. 57–62). Plants with adaptations will be best for your low-water garden.

Conditions causing the greatest water loss

Transpiration increases mainly when the atmosphere around the leaf is dry, conditions are hot, and there is considerable wind movement.

On a cloudless day transpiration increases rapidly in the morning, peaks just after the middle of the day, and declines to a minimum at night. Where water is readily available this process can continue, but in more stressful conditions a reduction in transpiration occurs earlier in the day, and may begin to be evident in the morning. However, this reduction in water loss is accompanied by a reduction in the rate of photosynthesis, and thus a reduction in growth rate.

Plant origins

Some plants have an enormous natural range. In Australia the most widely distributed eucalypt is the wonderful *Eucalyptus camaldulensis* (River Red Gum). This varies from almost prostrate but still large trees to huge bold-spreading trees and taller rather sparse trees. In Victoria their character changes, being particularly massive around Cavendish (south and south-west of the Grampians), whereas further north they are broad-headed trees of shorter stature.

Plants of a species that grow through a gradient of rainfall (areas from relatively low to very low rainfall) will have different tolerances to drought. Those originating in areas of moderate rainfall may not tolerate extreme drought as well as of those from the driest habitat.

The different zones where plants originate are called provenances, and the provenance of a plant will significantly affect its drought tolerance.

An English plant-collector would collect seed from plants in cold or frosty conditions but with high rainfall to suit the English climate. An Australian plant-hunter would obtain seeds from a hot, dry location. In other words, collectors should seek out different provenances of plants to obtain that which best suits their own home climate.

Many of the plants introduced to Australia from, say, California came via England; the English collectors rarely collected from suitable provenances for Australia. Californian plants like *Garrya elliptica* (Tassel Tree) or the beautiful *Fremontodendron californicum* (Flannel Bush) may not have been introduced from provenances compatible to Australia.

On the other hand, plants with a restricted natural distribution have limited genetic variation. It is likely that the plants will have similarities, no matter which sample is collected. This will be the case with the beautiful *Carpentaria californica* (Bush Anemone), which grows naturally on sunny slopes and ridges in restricted areas of the Sierra Nevada.

We should also be aware of the provenances of Australian flora. When establishing vegetation to extend or re-establish bush, use indigenous plants (plants of the local provenance). This is not so important for home gardeners, but at least choose plants from a compatible dry area.

Annuals

Ageratum hybrids	*
Althaea rosea (biennial)	*
Arctotis hybrids	**
Calendula officinalis	*
Centaurea cineraria	*
Cosmos bipinnatus	*
Helichrysum bracteatum	**
Lobularia maritima	**
Portulaca grandiflora	**
Sanvitalia procumbens	*
Tagates cvs	*

Plants in groups

Plants do not generally occur as mono-cultures in their native habitat, rather they are members of an overall association suited to their environment and its ecology (including soils, climate, and the animals and plants existing there). All of the plants in a particular association are able to exist, if not prosper, in the conditions of that habitat.

Parallels can be drawn with the home garden. Plants grown together in a single planting area should be considered not as individuals but as associations; though they may not grow together in associations naturally, they need to have similar tolerances and requirements in the garden. This is particularly true of their water demand, but they should also have similar tolerances of soil, sun, shade, wind, and so on.

To ensure that the final design is attractive, combine plants for colour and foliage interest (see the next chapter).

Consider the major differences between Mediterranean-climate gardens and those of the world's cool temperate regimes. Growth in the latter generally takes place between the last cold period at the end of winter or early spring and the first cold period of the autumn or early winter. In other words, the factor that controls growth is the cold. While cold may be a limiting factor in some areas, it is more likely that the limiting factor in Mediterranean environments will be water, or a lack of it.

Growth takes place when water is available (through the late winter and spring, possibly into early summer), but as summer advances and the environment becomes increasingly dry there is less growth; water stress will check growth. Indeed, in Melbourne in late summer hot northerly winds, with temperatures over 40°C, will cause a water loss, and may cause considerable damage to plants. It is quite noticeable that the Australian flowering season tends to be quite compressed, with the bulk of flowering in late spring and early summer. Some late-season plants do well, including both Australian plants (e.g. *Euycalyptus ficifolia* (Flowering Gum)), and introduced (e.g. *Plumbago auriculata* (Cape Plumbago) and *Agapanthus praecox* ssp. *orientalis* (Lily of the Nile)), but compared with say, the length of flowering in the cooler, gentler climate of the United Kingdom, the main flowering season is quite short. The general lack of frosts in Australia permits a more extensive range of plants to be cultivated, however.

Eucalypt leaves show adaptations to reduce water loss.

Watering can be habit-forming

In many respects the major problem of home gardens is that supplementary watering has been so easily available. Low-cost watering systems have made it possible for everybody to water their garden. This is not desirable from the viewpoint of plants. Watering outside the normal growth period of these dry-land plants extends their growth season. Where once their normal cycle of growth for which they are adapted resulted in a halt to growth as summer arrived, they now continue to grow.

This vigorous growth will have two effects. Firstly, plants will grow more quickly, possibly resulting in a shorter life. Secondly, watering may well lead to extended vigorous growth, fine while water is available to meet the transpiration rate of the plant, but a problem where water cannot be supplied to meet this demand. Towards the end of the summer, when water stress is greatest and growth is lushest, the highest temperatures may be experienced. Drying winds and intense solar energy are very damaging to plants.

Provide irrigation to plants only as a supplement to ensure their survival, to maintain existing growth and to compensate for being established in gardens at a higher density than might be the case in natural systems. Do not apply luxuriant quantities of water to obtain vigorous growth; it will increase your work, shorten the life of plants, and may lead to plant stress towards the end of summer, and a higher water bill.

Find out about low-water plants

Successful horticulture and garden design is largely based on good observation, on noticing how good two plants appear together, on experiencing the effects of particular spaces or the restfulness of particular colour schemes. You can learn a lot about the drought tolerance of plants, too, by observation.

In many places little water is applied to very large gardens or cemeteries, yet plants grow successfully. Many prosper extremely well, producing abundant flowers and foliage.

Some plants may naturalise too. Small isolated pockets of exotic plants sometimes occur in a roadside reserve, indicating the ability of these plants to grow without more than the natural rainfall. I have seen pockets of *Gladiolus tristis*, *Lilium candidum* (Madonna Lily) and *Zantedeschia aethiopica* (Arum Lily) all growing quite contentedly in this way. You may find, though, that they are growing in the moistest part of these reserves, in a permanently damp low spot.

Environmental weeds

The Australian bush is being taken over by a number of weeds ('garden escapes') that particularly suit the conditions present in the Australian environment. Not all of these weeds are introductions from abroad, some of our own plants, grown beyond their natural distribution, have escaped and now cause problems in the bush. Some of these are weeds of the home garden — my own site has produced seedlings of the *Pittosporum undulatum* (Sweet Pittosporum), while others are weeds of native bushland.

While you may consider weeds of your garden a sufficient problem, these problems are magnified many times over in the bush: weeds climb through the half-dead remnants of native trees, and cover the ground so completely that

Avoid spreading weeds

To ensure that you do not worsen the situation with weeds in bush near you, do not grow plants recognised as weeds in your area. Any plants that you tip into your bush may grow there; after all, if they've grown well in your garden, they'll probably grow well in the bush.

Either compost your prunings well so that you can use them as mulch, or seal them in plastic bags; put them in the sun and cook them before placing them in your garbage. *Never throw them into the bush.*

Be particularly careful about growing any plants producing berries, which make attractive food for birds or mammals. Having eaten the fruit, they can spread the seed throughout the bush, not only in areas of easy access but also in more remote areas. This process is evident in Sydney, where currawongs have been responsible for spreading *Ligustrum* sp. (Privet) and *Pittosporum undulatum* (Sweet Pittosporum) far and wide through the bush, while on the North Coast of New South Wales native pigeons have adopted *Cinnamomum camphora* (Camphor Laurel) as a primary food, and spread its seeds through the bush.

they preclude the germination of indigenous plants. At the same time, it is expensive to clear out these weeds and restore the native vegetation.

While as individual gardeners you may not directly be able to influence these existing weed covers (unless you decide to join a local group of enthusiasts working to control them), try not to add to this problem by discarding your rubbish unwisely.

Because we select plants for our dryland garden that suit our environment well and prosper on little effort by us, these very same plants may become weeds in the bush by naturalising there.

Some plants are weeds in one place and not in another. Indeed, plants that are a weed in one place are sold in nurseries elsewhere (e.g. *Lantana camara* (Common Lantana)). This plant is not only a weed throughout enormous areas of bush in New South Wales and Queensland, and has had a devastating impact on Norfolk Island, but it also is toxic to stock. *Lavandula stoechas* (Spanish Lavender), for example, is a weed of improved lands and pastures through South Australia and Victoria, though it is grown in inner-city gardens.

By growing plants suited to our garden environment we are also growing plants suited to our broader environment. Clearly, those plants with significant demands for water are not likely to become weeds, for our bushlands would offer a hostile environment for them without supplementary watering. By contrast, plants with a low water demand succeed without it.

Not all plants tolerating low-water regimes necessarily become weeds. Country cemeteries have a range of plants that have grown without water and indeed with little attention, yet their populations have remained localised. Of course, these plants may yet become weeds in the future.

Plants introduced into Australia have frequently been removed from their natural predators, without which there is little to prevent their very rapid spread and little to control their rapid increase in numbers.

Always check that plants you propose to use in your garden are not weeds. Environmental weeds are available as ornamental plants in our nurseries, and are best left there. There are, after all, many other beautiful plants to grow.

Eucalyptus erythrocorys (Red-cap Gum) is a most decorative small tree with an informal shape, able to tolerate low water and coastal salt.

Planting for water-efficient gardens

Although rainfall harvesting and mulching help, the selection of the most suitable plants is the most vital step in establishing a water-efficient garden. This need not restrict your flair and inventiveness in designing gardens: plants have an enormous range of colour and texture from foliage and flowers, as well as exciting shapes and habits. Low-water plants are no different from normal plants, they just use water differently. Many are standard, old-fashioned favourites of our parents and grandparents.

Before you buy, learn something about the plants you choose: recognise their foibles, the way they change through the year, how awful they might look through the winter before their elegant summer flowering, or how their evergreen foliage remains a feature throughout the year. Too frequently people are disappointed by their plants because they don't stop to investigate all of the plants' qualities and faults. Don't be tempted to purchase a plant just because of its picture in a catalogue or book, find out about its peculiarities and benefits before you establish it in your own garden.

Selecting for flowers

This is the most obvious feature of garden plants, used to identify a plant, and also as the feature that we recall. Flowers are the source of strong colour in gardens, and thus dictate our decorative planting combinations. How do you identify the best flowering plants for your garden?

Length of display is most important. A plant that flowers throughout the year is a real bonus. Flowering intensity may change (it is likely to be greatest in the summer and decline through the winter) but any plant that offers this continuity must be a good choice. Compare two lavenders: *Lavandula angustifolia* (English Lavender) and *L. dentata* (French Lavender). The latter flowers every month of the year, while the former has a short, mid-summer flowering season. Based on flowers alone you would choose the French Lavender, though there are other issues to consider. Length of flowering display is most important when the plant you are considering is a permanent, structural planting, but it is less significant for many bulbs or display plants that have only a seasonal period of interest. With roses, for example, there are so many different cultivars with different flowering duration that, with care, you can identify the long-flowering forms. Among a large group like the roses there will be different degrees of tolerance to drought, so select one of the best on this basis.

Just because a plant produces an endless supply of flowers it doesn't mean that it is a perfect garden plant, or that it will suit your garden. Many hibiscuses

Nepeta × mussini (Catmint) is an ideal groundcover for roses and as a border to a path.

grow enormous flowers, and they are widely popular. I don't like them, but others love them. Clearly personal taste is significant. Important elements include the size and shape of the flower, and how the flowers grow. *Gaura lindheimeri* (Gaura) has small flowers, but in extravagant masses.

Designing with foliage

While flowers may be intermittent in their display, many plants have foliage with year-round interest, a consistent covering to walls and fences, an ongoing backdrop to plants of outstanding shape and habit, and a setting for colourful flowering displays. Concentrate on planting a number of evergreen plants, since this will give a permanence to your garden: no matter how fleeting flowering may be, the garden will have interesting masses and shapes throughout the year. Just as you select the best flowers for your garden, select choice foliage forms too. Nurseries have already done this in many cases, displaying plants notable for the size of their leaves or for foliage colour: this may be seasonal colour (typically autumn or spring), but it may be a change in colour (purple instead of green leaves, variegated instead of plain).

Many of the plants suited to the water-efficient garden have greyish or at least pale-green leaves, while others have dark, waxy leaves. These foliage forms are full of interest, and offer you a remarkable design opportunity. As dark leaves make excellent backdrop plantings, use them to form a setting for other plantings. Plants like *Cupressus macrocarpa* (Cypress) or *Escallonia macrantha* (Common Escallonia) are good for this. Such plantings are also useful windbreaks, especially in coastal areas where salt-tolerant background plants help to achieve a micro-climate for the whole garden.

As well as pruning to get the best flowers, prune to get the best foliage from a plant. As plants age, their foliage often becomes smaller and less interesting. Many eucalypts, as well as other species, bear especially beautiful young leaves. By pruning to rejuvenate the plant you can continue to enjoy young foliage beauty. Leaves have qualities of colour absent from flowers: they are frequently more subtle and delicate, and appear quite different when strongly illuminated by the sun; many are translucent and may reveal delicate veination.

Colour is only one of the many qualities of young foliage. Different shapes offer enormous opportunity for garden picture composition, blending the bold with the delicate, the dramatic with the recessive, while their surfaces often reveal hairiness or gloss, rugosity or a glistening sheen. These qualities, carefully selected, can be matched or contrasted to masonry or paving or a gravel mulch for charming combinations.

Stem and trunk character

As well as foliage and flowers, consider other qualities such as the colours of stems and trunks. The grey leaves of *Eucalyptus polyanthemos* (Red Box) are enhanced by its coral-pink leaf petioles, while the trunk colour of the *Eucalyptus citriodora* (Lemon-scented Gum) varies from grey-silver through to delightful rosy pinks. A very high proportion of native Australian trees have beautiful bark.

Used as a focus, all these aspects can contribute in a really telling way to the garden. Don't use only a single trunk, mass them to create delightful thickets of repeated colour. In some circumstances, use them as geometric elements, the repetition of their trunks will provide a consistent and beautiful reference point, while in informal groups trunks create a sense of depth, of a forest thicket. You could mulch the ground with a mass of foliage. Shadow patterns of trunks and foliage on fences are a pleasing effect too.

Plants with scales and hairs

gc = groundcover; p = perennial;
s = shrub
Drought tolerance: *** (high)
**, * (good)

Artemisia pycnocephala	s **
Cineraria maritima	p **
Convolvulus cneorum	gc *
Helichrysum petiolare	p *
Juniperus sabina 'Tamariscifolia'	s **
Lavandula dentata	s **
Leucophyta brownii	s **
Phlomis fruticosa	s *
Stachys byzantina	p, gc *

Drought-tolerant emergents

gc = groundcover; p = perennial;
s = shrub
Drought tolerance: *** (high)
**, * (good)

Agave attenuata	***
Aloe arborescens	***
Anigozanthos flavidus	*
A. manglesii	*
Cordyline australis	**
Dietes bicolor	**
D. iridioides	**
Kniphofia uvaria	**
Phormium tenax	**
Strelitzia reginae	**
Yucca recurvifolia	***
Y. whipplei	***

ABOVE: James Hitchmough's delightful garden was designed specifically as a low-water garden. A drip watering system was used with low-water demanding plants, heavy mulch, and gravel in preference to lawn. (PHOTO: JOHN PATRICK)

RIGHT: Paul Thompson designed this fine garden in Templestowe (Vic.) to collect water from all surfaces, including the driveway and paths, and to fill a system of ponds through the garden. The ponds dry out in summer, but for much of the year they are a haven for birds. The garden has become the inspiration for many other local gardeners, who have now established a wildlife corridor. (PHOTO: PAUL THOMPSON)

BELOW RIGHT: Economical use of water is essential where water is scarce. A simple bowl of clear water is a refreshing sight. (PHOTO: GEOFF SANDERSON)

ABOVE: Dry conditions in Australia result partly from the intense heat and light of the sun. Protection by a canopy of trees also gives attractive shadow patterns. The gravel mulch permits easy movement around the garden, and a contrast of textures to foliage and surface. (PHOTO: LORNA ROSE)

LEFT: Lawn was replaced by groundcover plants, including thymes, in this charming back yard in Castlemaine (Vic.). Water running through the garden collects in a small pond, which waxes and wanes with available water. (PHOTO: JOHN PATRICK)

BELOW LEFT: *Euphorbia robbiae* is one of those valuable plants that grows in dry shade. (PHOTO: JOHN PATRICK)

BELOW: *Eschscholzia californica* is one of the most dependable and exciting of low-water annuals. (PHOTO: JOHN PATRICK)

ABOVE: Grey foliage plants generally have excellent drought tolerance, but grow best in sun. *Macleaya cordata* (Plume Poppy) and the New Zealand native *Euphorbia glauca* provide outstanding textural interest. (PHOTO: JOHN PATRICK)

ABOVE RIGHT: The grey foliage and pink flowers of this *Arctotis* sp. make it extremely attractive. (PHOTO: JOHN PATRICK)

RIGHT: *Gladiolus × colvillei* is an excellent addition to a spring garden. It naturalises to provide large clumps of angled flower spikes. (PHOTO: JOHN PATRICK)

BELOW: Careful combination of low-water plants can achieve beautiful effects. Here it is *Echinacea purpurea* with the elegant *Verbena bonariensis*. Silver *Artemisia arborescens* (Shrubby Artemisia) is a suitable backdrop. (PHOTO: JOHN PATRICK)

ABOVE LEFT: The silver foliage of *Artemisia* is a fine foil, both texturally and in colour, for other plants, in this case a red-flowered sage. (PHOTO: ROBIN POWELL)

ABOVE: Kangaroo Paws are among the most exciting of low-water plants. Their textures are attractive in this combination with a grass tree. (PHOTO: ROBIN POWELL)

LEFT: The emergent spikes of *Kniphofia* 'Winter Torch' (Red-hot Poker) add texture and majestic flower-heads, a delightful focus to any garden. (PHOTO: JOHN PATRICK)

BELOW LEFT: Mown grass occupies a limited part of this garden. Beyond, longer grass is allowed to dry off. It offers an attractive contrast in texture. Low native plants soften the steps and include *Wahlenbergia gloriosa* and *Prostanthera saxicola* var. *montana*. Note that chipped wood provides both a step and a mulch. (PHOTO: RODGER ELLIOT)

Shape and structure

Whether you use these trees as informal masses or as geometric formal grids depends very much on the type of plant involved. Formal plants, like mop-head robinias are well suited to grid-like planting, whereas informal plants, such as the beautiful *Allocasuarina torulosa* (Forest Oak) suit loose groupings. The shape and growth habit of the plant help you to decide, though there are some plants that suit both planting approaches (e.g. lavenders can be planted as a loose massing or as a clipped hedge).

The structure of a plant differs from the outer shape of foliage and branches of a plant: the beautifully coloured flowering *Myoporum floribundum* has a layered habit, and the *Schinus molle* var. *areira* (Peppercorn) a weeping one. This may be striking, but can be very difficult to use in design.

You can create strong shapes in a garden by clipping plants (e.g. box hedges or pyramids of box) at critical locations.

Don't allow plants of strong shapes and habits to disrupt your garden design. The shape of a plant is often lost when plants are massed, the individual tree submerged within the whole planting, rather than being seen as a single specimen.

Ornamental fruit

What a bonus fruit provide, not only for their colour and form but also for the way they attract birds to the garden. Many plants produce most attractive fruits, extending their ornamental display. The fruit can hang on the plant for a long time, though they may also offer a decorative cover on the ground (e.g. the yellow fruit of lemons look splendid lying on a lawn).

Decorative fruit drop onto the ground and are a nuisance to some people. The fruit can be raked up quite easily, and are often no more than a slight inconvenience. The fruit of lemons, many of the hawthorns and the persimmons are especially beautiful. Choose plants with an ability to hold their fruit well. Remember that fruit are the sources of seed for plants, so they have the potential to distribute the plant, and this may not be desirable.

Scent effects

Perfumes of plants are indeed most pleasurable, though this seems to have been more fully appreciated in the past than it is today: the strewing of scented plants on floors, a continuation of a Roman tradition, overcame other less pleasant smells. Fortunately for the Romans their native plants included several with wonderful scents: thymes, lavenders, sages and rosemaries native to dry slopes of the Mediterranean. Some had beautifully fragrant flowers (e.g. lavenders), oils from the foliage of others smelt wonderful. These oils may have had a role in overcoming competition from adjacent plants or of reducing water loss from leaves by creating a changed atmosphere around the leaf surface.

You can enjoy the same effects in your garden: use, say, a hedge of rosemary where you can touch it to release the perfume, or herbs such as thyme as a beautifully scented lawn. This is best where space is restricted, it can involve a lot of weeding for the best results.

It is said, and I suspect from my experience it may be so, that the strongest scents emanate from plants grown in the most stressed environments, that is, with low-water and low-fertiliser regimes.

Plants with scented foliage

gc = groundcover; p = perennial; s = shrub; t = tree
Drought tolerance: *** (high)
**, * (good)

Aloysia triphylla (*Lippia citriodora*)	s	**
Artemisia absinthium	s	***
Citrus sp.	s	**
Eucalyptus (many)	t	
E. citriodora	t	***
Laurus nobilis	t	**
Lavandula angustifolia	s	**
L. dentata	s	**
Myrtus communis	t	**
Nepeta × *faassenii*	gc	**
Pelargonium (many)	p	**
Rosmarinus officinalis	s	**
Ruta graveolens	s	*
Salvia officinalis	s	*
Santolina chamaecyparissus	s	*
Thymus vulgaris	gc	**

Yucca whipplei has remarkable shape and habit. I especially enjoy the contrast between the light colour of the leaf tips and the shade at the centre of the foliage.

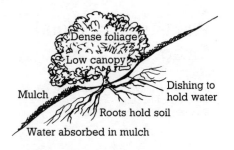

Erosion reduced by plants with dense foliage and fibrous roots.

Design with plants

Given this list of qualities of plants, you now need to combine them to achieve the best effects. Plants have both a visual quality (flower colour or foliage form) and a functional quality (screening, creating windbreaks or shade). (See Further reading for more detailed accounts.) Windbreaks and shade creation have been discussed in relation to garden micro-climate (page 9). Let us now consider some other requirements.

Soil stability

Plants provide an ideal way of reducing soil erosion because they intercept rainfall and through their roots stabilise the soil surface. This is vitally important on sloping sites.

The worst situation is to have a finely tilled soil overlaid upon a hard (rocky) base, for this is very easily eroded. It is better to leave the soil less well broken down, to use a water-absorbing mulch and plants with a fibrous root system to bind the surface.

Grass has frequently been used for this purpose but it is not easy to maintain, especially as slopes become steeper, and it is high in its water demands. It is better to use low shrub massings, which need little pruning and are often more decorative and less water-demanding.

Select plants that intercept the rainfall and reduce its speed before it strikes the soil surface by holding it on the branches and releasing it slowly (dense foliage is vital here), and augment these with a good mulch.

Where conditions on the slope are especially difficult, either plant in pockets of soils irrigated by drip-irrigation systems, or encourage climbing plants to tumble down the slope. *Hibbertia scandens* (Climbing Guinea Flower), hardenbergias and many other climbers do this very effectively.

Screening and enclosure

As inner-city gardens become smaller and buildings encroach on garden spaces, the need for screening to achieve privacy becomes greater. This should not occupy too much space in your garden. Unlike masonry and other structures, plants don't achieve an immediate screen, but they can be effective if you have the necessary patience.

Combine a plant with a structure, half fence and half hedge, for the best results. A tall screen will inevitably give some shade, and this may be a distinct disadvantage to either you or your neighbour. Your council may have planning controls covering structures that provide a screen, but there are no controls on planted screens; respect your neighbour's needs.

Screening also provides a windbreak. However, the large leaf area of many screens could lead to a high water demand. It may be worthwhile having a root barrier to prevent screening plants with invasive roots from removing all of the water so essential for the cultivation of other plants.

If you need a screen in very limited space, why not cover a fence with climbers? *Pandorea pandorana* (Wonga Wonga Vine) in one of its many forms would be excellent; it offers strength and can be clipped. Otherwise, a hedge would be good. Where plants alone are used they can be space demanding. *Cupressus macrocarpa* (Monterey Cypress) forms a large dense hedge, a complete barrier. Study the form of hedge plants to ensure they are sufficiently dense; some plants do not grow together sufficiently to give a complete screen.

Weed suppression

Groundcovers suppress weed growth by shading out weeds and occupying weed space. This is a distinct benefit to water use but remember that your

Massing of trees, shrubs and groundcover for consistent visual impact.

weed suppressant also has a water demand (though it is prettier). Ground-covers shade the soil, so they affect evaporation rates from the surface, and may save water. The ground must be clean before weed-suppressing ground-covers are established or the weeds will simply grow through, making main-tenance even more difficult. Perennials, especially, must be planted in clean ground, otherwise the plants become inextricably interwoven.

Design for beauty

Functional roles aside, most plants are grown for their beauty, though other plants are grown for the crops they produce, either as herbs, fruit or vegetables. In ornamental planting, design plants in a series of layers, from the tallest trees to the lowest groundcovers. Clearly, the larger trees have the greatest impact: choose single specimens (or, if you have a very large garden, in extensive blocks or drifts), with smaller plants in larger blocks. The modern tendency is towards sizeable drifts of plants for the greatest effect.

We will now consider each of the groups of plants in turn to assess their role and impact in design, and their effect on the low-water garden.

Trees

These vary enormously in size. While I believe suburbs need large trees to create a sense of scale, you may not need a large one in your garden. If you already have a very large tree ask yourself whether you should keep it. It will certainly use a lot of water, but it will provide shade for other plants. However, large trees can be misery to live with, and you may choose to remove it. Consider your options carefully and take advice, but do realise that trees have a finite life. If the tree is over-mature it may be best to remove it. The tree may perhaps give you important privacy, however, and its removal could leave you exposed; you could thin it instead to achieve the same benefits. Do not employ tree loppers, find a sensitive and well-qualified tree surgeon.

Trees provide shade and shelter, flowers, foliage, fruit and bark displays, and their shape and habit can be important to your garden design. As well, their mass is significant. The shade they create can cause complications by shading grass or other plants, or by competing. Remember that trees planted to the southern end of your site will shade your neighbours' garden, but will leave your plants in the sun to flower and develop well.

Trees shading your patio or house will effectively modify the temperature of your environment, so select them carefully. Trees can establish and frame viewlines through your garden, by massing them you will have a wonderful woodland habitat with repeated trunks. Always choose a tree suited to your soils and rainfall. Some trees can be unstable on clay soils, so ensure that they root deeply; break up the soil and irrigate deeply.

For useful information on selecting trees, consult Further reading.

Shrubs

These are enormously variable woody plants with either a multi-trunked or a low-branching character, and they range from low groundcovers like junipers and cotoneasters through to large plants with enormous numbers of branches and extensive foliage cover, like buddleias. Being so diverse in their shape and character, shrubs are also diverse in their properties. Some are grown for their foliage, such as the *Nandina domestica* (Japanese Sacred Bamboo) — nothing to do with real bamboo — though it does flower and produce handsome red berries in coolish climates. Roses are obviously grown for their flowers and

Helianthemum mummularium (Rock Rose) produces prolific flowers when planted in sun. It is one of the best low-water groundcovers.

Trees for dry conditions

Drought tolerance: *** (high)
**, * (good)

Acacia melanoxylon	*
A. pendula	**
A. stenophylla	**
Agonis flexuosa	**
Albizia julibrissin	**
Allocasuarina torulosa	**
Angophora costata	***
Arbutus unedo	*
Brachychiton populneus	***
Calocedrus decurrens	*
Casuarina cristata	***
Cedrus atlantica	*
Celtis australis	**
Ceratonia siliqua	***
Cupressus sempervirens	**
Elaeagnus angustifolia	*
Eucalyptus lehmanii	**
E. nicholii	**
E. papuana	***
Genista aetnensis	*
Gleditsia triacanthos	**
Jacaranda mimosifolia	*
Lagerstroemia indica	*
Magnolia grandiflora	*
Melia azedarach	**
Metrosideros excelsa	*
Morus alba	**
Myrtus communis	**
Pinus bungeana	*
P. pinea	**
Pittosporum phylliraeoides	**
Quercus ilex	***
Robinia pseudoacacia	**
Schinus terebinthifolius	***
S. molle var. *areira*	**

scent, and only occasionally for foliage, though *Rosa glauca*, with grey leaves and handsome red hips, is one exception. Given this range it is no surprise to find that they are subdivided into different categories.

Buffer shrubs

These large background shrubs give better enclosure than trees, which may be quite open along their trunks and have only higher lateral branches. By contrast, shrubs often have lower branches, unless these branches are shaded out (e.g. camellias, coastal rosemaries and oleanders). This makes them especially effective at screening boundaries or fences. Many can be secured to fences, either as espalier plants or as loose hedges; *Camellia sasanqua* (Sasanqua Camellia) may be handled in either way. Buffer shrubs are generally used for background planting, though their size may make them ill-suited for smaller gardens. Many produce voluminous masses of foliage and wood for the degree of flower production (e.g. *Vitex agnus-castus* (Chaste Tree)), but others are very floriferous. Some shrubs can be cut back very hard to rejuvenate them; they then grow very fast because of their established root systems (e.g. buddleias, oleanders, etc.) As background plants they are frequently used as a foil for other ornamental plantings, especially if they have small, dark foliage; this gives increased depth to a garden design.

Feature shrubs

These shrubs (usually 1–2.5 metres high) provide middle-ground interest. There is usually space for these shrubs in a garden. They contribute to the garden scheme because of their mass, and because their scale is comfortable for garden users. They are usually planted closer to the front of planting schemes; in small gardens they may be the predominant element. The appearance of their flowers and foliage is therefore important because they will be closely inspected and enjoyed; choose plants with good foliage texture and enduring flower display. Many roses, in spite of their extensive flower display, do not have good texture and form. Select those with the longest flowering; if they have poor structure and appearance, surround them with screening plants to disguise their faults.

Because of their size, you may need to plant multiples of feature shrubs to achieve an effective mass against buffer shrubs and trees.

Sub-shrubs

Treat these woody plants as elements of herbaceous perennial plantings; in their size and form they are generally viewed as part of the herbaceous perennial scheme. Where they are surrounded by tall shrubs or herbaceous plants they often become drawn up, and need to be cut back consistently to obtain new growth.

Many well-known shrubs are classed as sub-shrubs: lavenders, cotton-lavenders, the smaller hebes and scaevolas. To create an effect these plants should be massed; their size makes them well suited to this. They are also good grown in masses with emergent foliage plants to produce textural combinations.

Groundcover shrubs

These can be extremely useful where large massings of groundcovers are required. Use plants such as *Cotoneaster* 'Skogholm' or *Grevillea* 'Poorinda Royal Mantle' for low-maintenance and low-water covers. Not all are dense groundcovers, and they don't always combine well with emergent plants. A few are useful as individual feature shrubs in the right place (e.g. *Juniperus*

Drought-tolerant shrubs & sub-shrubs

Drought tolerance: *** (high)
                    **, * (good)

Banksia ericifolia	**
Buddleia davidii	*
Caesalpinia gilliesii	*
Carpentaria californica	**
Ceanothus species	**
Ceratostigma willmottianum	*
Chamelaucium uncinatum	**
Choisya ternata	*
Correa alba	**
C. 'Dusky Bells'	**
Cistus species	**
Dodonaea viscosa	**
Echium fastuosum	**
Euphorbia characias ssp. *wulfenii*	**
Euryops pectinatus	**
Fremontodendron californicum	**
Garrya elliptica 'James Roof'	**
Hibiscus syriacus	*
Jasminum mesnyi	*
Kolkwitzia amabilis	*
Lavandula angustifolia	**
L. dentata	*
L. pinnata	***
Leonotis leonurus	**
Nerium oleander	***
Osmanthus fragrans	**
Perovskia atriplicifolia	**
Pittosporum tobira	**
Plumbago auriculata	**
Prostanthera baxteri	*
Prunus ilicifolia	***
Raphiolepis indica	***
R. umbellatam	***
Russelia equisetiformis	*
Salvia leucantha	**
Tecoma stans	**
Teucrium fruticans	**
Viburnum tinus	**
Vitex agnus-castus	***
Westringia 'Wynyabbie Gem'	**

horizontalis (Horizontal Juniper), while it is classified as a groundcover it could be classified as a feature shrub).

This group of plants is most useful for low-maintenance gardens. By careful selection you will have a garden of shrubs providing colour and interest with a minimum need for clipping, division or culling, and relatively easily irrigated with drip irrigation.

Herbaceous perennials

These deciduous or evergreen plants lack the woody structure of shrubs. They are invaluable because of their remarkably diverse tolerances. Some are able to tolerate shade, others full sun; some tolerate open sandy soils, others heavy clays; some drought, others waterlogging.

Again, they are so numerous that they need to be considered in distinct groups.

Emergents

These are among the most important of garden design plants because they offer so much of interest. By selecting plants with especially striking form you will create attractive assemblages with contrasting leaf forms. The emergent plant must grow through the lower surrounding plants, however.

Suitable plants include many grasses and grass-like plants (e.g. *Doryanthes palmeri* (Spear Lily), *Miscanthus sinensis* (Japanese Silver Grass) and *Phormium tenax* (New Zealand Flax) and the many bulbous or rhizomatous plants with this leaf structure (e.g. *Dierama pulcherrimum* (Fairy Fishing Rod), *Dietes grandiflora* (South African Iris) and *Orthrosanthus multiflorus* (Morning Flag)).

These plants look good also in combination with paving textures and gravel mulches. They are equally effective planted as bold drifts.

Groundcovers

As the name suggests, these herbaceous perennial plants cover ground and suppress weeds. Some plants form large clumps so that they occupy the space, others form mounds of foliage, covering a large area. A number produce rhizomes, and cover the ground by shooting at points along the roots; others tip shoot as they grow, producing many little plants. These are most useful if they are evergreen, since year-round cover is essential.

Herbaceous groundcovers have real value for the flexibility of form that woody covers frequently lack. The best have good foliage texture and form for combining with adjacent planting. These plants should be massed to provide a horizontal area between plants.

Evergreen and deciduous free form

Perennials include an enormous range of plants. The deciduous forms leave gaps in a garden, which is not always welcome, but Australia's mild winters are so short that it is not the great disadvantage it is in other countries.

The great qualities of these plants are their variable sizes, flower forms and colours so that, in association with shrubs and sub-shrubs, they provide an enormous range of colour and interest. Well chosen, there are no finer garden plants; no wonder they are popular. However, they are under-utilised in most gardens.

Annuals and biennials

You can create patches of seasonal display colour with these. They are especially well suited to specific garden locations where a splash of colour is essen-

Drought-tolerant groundcovers

Drought tolerance: *** (high)
**, * (good)

Ajuga reptans	*
Asteriscus maritimus	**
Ceanothus griseus 'Yankee Point'	**
Convolvulus mauritanicus	**
Coprosma × *kirkii*	**
Erigeron karvinskianus	**
Felicia amelloides	*
Gazania cvs	***
Genista hispanica	**
Grevillea aquifolium	**
G. 'Poorinda Royal Mantle'	*
Helianthemum nummularium cvs	**
Hypericum calycinum	**
Juniperus horizontalis	**
J. sabina 'Tamariscifolia'	**
Lampranthus aurantiacus cvs	**
Leptospermum 'Horizontalis'	
Liriope spicata	*
Lonicera pileata	*
Myoporum parvifolium	**
Nepeta × *faassenii*	**
Ophiopogon japonicus	**
Osteospermum fruticosum	**
Ruscus aculeatus	***
R. hypoglossum	**
Scaevola 'Mauve Clusters'	**
Teucrium chamaedrys	*
Thymus pseudolanuginosus	*
Zauschneria californica	**

Bulbs, corms, tubers & rhizomes

Drought tolerance: *** (high)
**, * (good)

Amaryllis belladonna	***
Bulbine bulbosa	*
Canna cv.	**
Clivia miniata	*
Colchicum autumnale	*
C. speciosum	**
Crinum flaccidum	**
Cyclamen hederifolium	**
Gladiolus × *colvillei* 'The Bride'	*
G. natalensis	*
G. tristis	*
Ipheion uniflorum	***
Lilium candidum	**
Scilla peruviana	**
Sternbergia lutea	**
Tulipa saxatilis	**
Watsonia alethroides	**

Drought-tolerant climbers

Drought tolerance: *** (high)
**, * (good)

Bougainvillea glabra and cvs	**
Campsis radicans	**
Ficus pumila	**
Gelsemium sempervirens	*
Hardenbergia comptoniana	**
H. violacea	**
Hoya carnosa	**
Jasminum polyanthum	*
Macfadyena unguis-cati	*
Parthenocissus quinquefolia	*
Pyrostegia venusta	**
Rosa banksiae	**
Sollya heterophylla	**
Tecomaria capensis	**

tial, or in tubs and hanging baskets. Because many have relatively restricted root development they are susceptible to low water levels (e.g. *Impatiens*), and are frequently the first to show evidence of drought. These display plantings should be in sufficiently tight groups to provide a continual canopy over the ground to minimise water loss by evaporation. Use mulches; their restricted area means that even a little extra watering will not add significantly to the water budget.

Bulbs

Bulbs do not take up too much space or gardener's effort. They are enormously variable in form, including corms, bulbs, tubers, and, in the broadest sense, rhizomes.

Bulbs can provide massed groundcover effects (e.g. *Cyclamen hederifolium* (Dwarf Cyclamen) or textured emergent masses (e.g. *Gladiolus* × *colvillei* 'The Bride'). Others give low-maintenance massing (e.g. *Agapanthus praecox* ssp. *orientalis* (Lily of the Nile)).

The good news for the water-efficient gardener is that a number of bulbs will grow in low-water environments — one reason the bulbous root evolved was to survive low water.

Climbing plants

Climbing plants are very adaptable; they can be trained to descend or become horizontal. Their descending quality makes them useful as groundcovers, either pegged down or allowed to root at nodes, while their climbing capacity is well known. They can be self-clinging (*Parthenocissus* spp.), twiners (wisterias), tendrils (sweet peas) or hooks (bougainvilleas). Some don't have great adaptations for climbing but produce effusive growth that simply lies on other plants (e.g. climbing roses).

Because they grow from shade into sun, they generally appreciate a moist root environment (e.g. from a drip watering system).

With careful placement of climbers a garden can be enclosed, especially if the plants are grown over lattice or wire frames.

Planting groups

You can learn much about plants by observation, preferably by viewing them in garden settings or nurseries. Find the best local nursery for good advice about the tolerances and performances of plants.

The best way to design with plants is to identify what you want in a plant (height, spread, colour, foliage, character, etc.) and then choose the appropriate plant. Too frequently home gardeners buy on impulse at a nursery, either because a plant is in flower, or it is being promoted, or it is in just the right spot in the nursery. None are sound reasons. Buy a plant because it meets your garden design needs, not on impulse.

Good planting design comes from working out exactly what you want: for example, a shrub to three metres, with blue flowers and evergreen greyish foliage, or a round-leaved evergreen, groundcovering perennial to be used as a foil for a sword-leaved emergent. By choosing in this way you establish guidelines for what you will buy from the nursery.

Always go pre-armed with as much information as possible. Go through a good plant book (the *Reader's Digest Encyclopaedia of Garden Plants* is a great place to start) and list all the plants that suit your needs, so that you have a choice. Consider the plant not only individually but also how it will look in groups or against its neighbours. It is always sensible to have a few options.

From a viewpoint of water-efficiency, all the plants in a group should have similar water requirements. Selecting compatible plants suited to dry locations will be an advantage, especially if you use grey foliage schemes against a background of dark green.

Colour your design

Colour is probably the most significant feature of your garden. We all tend to select plants with especially colourful foliage or flowers. For many people gardens mean flowers.

Colour also comes from paving, from paint (on garden furniture and lattice), from sculptures, and possibly from glazed tiles in ornamental ponds, but plant colour is likely to be the dominant aspect of most people's gardening. Just as you use colour to establish mood and decoration inside your house, so too it decorates the outside, creating mood in your garden.

Colour use in the garden is slightly different from internal colour. The tendency indoors is to use large areas of a single colour, whereas external colour tends to be rather more broken. Choose an association of colours carefully for contrast and harmony. Colour in the garden is also subject to intense sunlight. Some gardeners use quiet pastel colours effectively, but in contrast just visualise the splendour of massed heads of blue agapanthuses in full sun.

Harmonious colour schemes include closely related colours so the range of colours will be relatively limited. Pinks with soft blues create a quiet, soft harmony, perfect for a location where you wish to relax. This is a safe solution. If you take a little more risk, the colour scheme can be more powerful. The harmony is retained but the quietness of the first scheme has been made more exciting.

Harmony may still be achieved with even stronger colours. For example, to the rich pinks of old roses add some of the dark and fulsomely flowered clematises, irises and herbaceous geraniums, and you will have a wonderfully rich and exciting harmony of colour.

Colours used for contrast are those removed from each other in the colour circle. Imagine a combination of the yellow of achilleas and evening primroses with the blues of agapanthuses or orthrosanthuses.

Plant spacing

One of the ways plants survive drought is by separating themselves from their neighbouring plants. Where they grow close together, of course, there is intense competition for water as conditions become drier; the danger is that plants will compete and become stressed. Productivity will be reduced. If this continues, the plants may eventually die.

The garden is not a natural system because we are able to apply supplementary water to avoid situations of extreme stress. But, inevitably, when we use plants in massed planting schemes there is competition between them, resulting in higher water use. As we do not wish to grow isolated plants in most garden settings, some competition is inevitable. The most successful plants will be those that establish themselves quickly, getting their root system into the ground and finding water early in their development. But water is only one of the vital resources for which plants will be competing. Quick root growth will also allow quick growth of foliage canopy; this will cause shading of adjacent plants, so that further advantage will be obtained. Prune as needed so that all plants grow as you wish.

How to assess plant quality

- Buy the plant from a nursery in which you have confidence: assess the information available from the nursery, the ability of the staff to advise you, and their general interest in selling you a plant. A nursery concerned about helping you will also be concerned about selling you a quality plant.
- Assess the plant in its container. Ensure that the balance between them is correct; in other words, avoid small pots containing enormous plants, and, conversely, large pots containing small plants; try to find the right balance.

    Lift the plant up by the plant, not the pot to ensure that the plant and soil are a good unit. If the plant lifts out of the pot and the soil collapses, then it is likely to have been grown in the open ground and potted up for sale. Don't buy this plant; you want a container-grown one!
- Look for an even glossy greenness of foliage. A healthy plant has a lustre (the equivalent of the cold, wet nose, glossy coat and clear eyes of a puppy).
- Check the extent of the new growth on the plant, you don't want a plant that has been forced by excessive applications of nitrogen to grow too quickly; be suspicious of excessive sappy growth.
- Check for any sign of pest infestation (black spot on roses or evidence of other diseases).
- Has the plant been sufficiently watered?
- Does it have good root development, not masses of roots coming from the base of the pot (it may have been too long in the pot)?

Colour effects

How can you use colour-contrast effects in the garden? Where you wish to sit and relax, use quiet colours; the quietest harmony of all is the extensive use of grey foliage, possibly with white flowers. This scheme is especially lovely in the evening. Many 'white' gardens are mostly of green foliage, but are still beautiful.

Though the white garden has been enormously popular, people now plan gardens with more colour and livelier planting schemes to suit an active garden. Where lively harmonies or contrasts are established, it becomes a garden of energy where children may play.

Separation of colour schemes may be by seasons, using a particular scheme for a particular season or, more frequently, separating them by space so that different parts of a garden have a different colour effect. Isn't that exactly what we do in our houses by use of different paint colours?

Without supplementary watering a dry soil will not be able to support dense plantings. As the plants grow, water will become scarce, and this will limit their size; it may eventually lead to their death.

Buy the best

When you plant your garden use the best quality plants available so that they establish themselves quickly. There is little benefit in nursing sickly plants. Select the best available plants: you pay a little more for the plants, but it is worthwhile.

We have already seen that plants develop shade and sun leaves. This is certainly the case with plants in a nursery, where they are kept in a shade house. Plants such as camellias are kept in these locations, together with many seedlings, and so on. This has implications for how you might look after the plants when you buy them. There is little value in obtaining the very best quality plants from your nursery if you then treat them poorly. If you transport them in an open windy position (e.g. on the back of an open vehicle), they will be subjected to the effects of drying winds; this will have a significant effect on their health. If you also fail to water plants sufficiently when you take them home from the nursery, you will find that they may become water stressed. Wean your plants over time from a high-water regime to a lower-water regime. Plants taken from shade and protection in the nursery, and then put into full sun in your garden, will inevitably suffer. Stand the pot in increasing levels of light over a period of time.

Not all of the plants you purchase will be grown in containers, though this has become more frequent in recent years. Some trees are still sold bare-rooted (e.g. ornamental apples and pears). This is an ideal way to obtain many of the deciduous trees at heights of 1–1.5 metres. Check that the trees have been stored correctly (with moist roots) throughout the whole time they were out of the ground. Obviously, the longer they are in the nursery the greater the likelihood that they will dry out, so ask the nursery to inform you when their stock first arrives so that you can make an early selection. Use wet hessian to keep the roots moist until you get the plants home and into the ground, most importantly ensuring that any air pockets are removed from the soil, and water them well.

Do you really need so much lawn?

The most water-demanding element of any garden is the lawn. Water-saving gardeners everywhere recognise this, and adjust the amount of lawn accordingly: for example, in Darwin water-saving gardens were created by omitting lawns altogether, while in Canberra three types of water-saving gardens have been created, from relatively high consumption to low consumption, the level of consumption being controlled by the amount of lawn used, from a relatively large area in the high consumption garden to very little in the xeriscape. To save water look very carefully at your lawns and consider whether you need them at all. In any case, ensuring that over-watering is avoided is critical because the application of excessive water is not only wasteful of water but may also lead to excessive growth, leaching of fertilisers, and an increase in disease and weed growth. Whatever your decision, the following issues are the most significant ones in relation to lawns and water use:

- lawn area and shape
- soil type
- grass type
- watering practices and frequency
- maintenance programmes.

The best lawn shape

There is much to be said for not having a lawn at all. If you want to save water ask yourself whether you need a lawn. Treat your lawn as a functional, not as an aesthetic, element of the garden. There is no doubt that a lawn is an ideal place for children or grandchildren to play, and as such is a desirable addition to any garden, but the area required for this can be quite limited. It is likely that you will wish this area of garden to be in your rear garden for privacy rather than in the front garden. There may be no benefit at all in using lawn in the front, it could be effectively replaced by a carpet of massed groundcovers offering a rich composition of textures and colours, or by a low-water native garden. The expectation for closely mown, evergreen lawns is widespread, yet it is one of the most visually sterile landscapes.

Many alternatives to lawns have a far lower tolerance of trampling than do lawn grasses, so you may still choose to use lawn for functional areas. In small gardens paving is a sensible alternative. If you have a small garden or perhaps a courtyard, ask yourself whether you wish to store a mower and undertake regular maintenance, or simply brush down a paved area.

If you decide that you do need a lawn, consider what is the most economical shape for water use. As already suggested, a circular lawn with a central

Chemical inhibition

Grasses also release chemical inhibitors, which can restrict both growth rates and cropping, so there may be distinct benefits in having less grass.

Lawn shapes

Lawn shapes have a significant effect on watering. A long narrow lawn has a perimeter to area ratio that is quite different from one where all sides are long. This ratio is an indicator of water consumption efficiency: the lower the ratio value, the greater the efficiency.

30 m | Perimeter = 120 m
30 m | Area = 900 sq. m
| Efficiency (p ÷ a) = 0.13

3 m | Perimeter = 63 m
1.5 m | Area = 45 sq. m
| Efficiency (p ÷ a) = 1.4

When the perimeter to area ratio is greater than 0.25, then the lawn is inefficient. Check yours, and make the necessary changes.

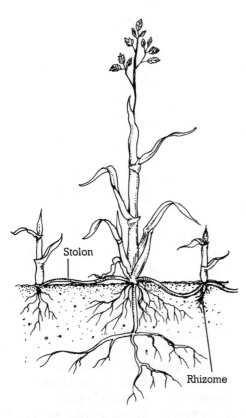

Stolon

Rhizome

Rhizomatous shoot system.

pop-up irrigation head is desirable (windy weather will cause some drift), but a circular lawn may not always fit your design. In general, flowing and complex lawn shapes result in water wastage when irrigation patterns overlap extensively and are lost to surrounding garden beds. Formal shapes need to be such that they are water-efficient, as calculated by establishing their perimeter to area ratio (see the side column examples). Turf at the edge of a lawn will dry out more quickly, especially next to paving where reflected heat increases the rate of evapotranspiration. It would be better to replace grass nature strips with massed, low-water groundcovers.

Lawn surfaces retain little moisture on slopes. Most water will run off, leaving the grass very dry and the base of the slope wet. It is preferable to retain a slope, with shrubs and a mulch, especially since this will also achieve good soil reinforcement and prevent erosion.

Soil type

The effects of soils on water have important implications for turf, not least is the effect of soil on water penetration. We all know the effects of too much rainfall on clay soils; without improved drainage water tends to pond on the surface of the grass. A similar effect occurs if water is added too quickly.

Ensure that water application rates match water penetration rates of your soil. With sandy soils this is not likely to be a problem, but apply water to clay soils as a series of short bursts rather than as a single continuous process, so that water is able to penetrate the soil. Remove any thatch (matting of debris or clippings) on clay soils; and aerate the soil.

At the outset make sure that your lawn is suitably established. This is most important on new home sites where builders may have left behind areas of compaction, stockpiles of waste material, large pieces of masonry from a demolished house, etc. Rip through any compacted layers, and remove rubble. Cultivate any sand into the soil (the sand may impede water movement). Test whether gypsum is needed, and check the pH of the soil, applying lime if the soil is too acid and inhibiting activity of decomposing fungi. If you have a heavy clay soil, add a sandy loam, mixing it at their interface, and implement any necessary drainage. You could mix a coarse sand with your clay to improve soil structure.

What grass is best?

As for other types of plants, grasses vary in their tolerance of drought: some grasses can be allowed to dry out completely and will grow back as soon as rains occur, while other grasses are most intolerant of drought. If you are going to have an area of grass, choose plants with a good tolerance of low water.

Why not use the approach of allowing grass to dry out completely, to die off and then to re-grow when water is available, to at least the outer zones of your garden? Grasses with a rhizomatous root formation (such as Couch, Blue Couch, and Chewing's Fescue) are best suited to this treatment.

Lawn grasses are divided into two types: cool season and warm season. Cool-season grasses grow mostly in the cool part of the year, but are not very efficient in terms of water use. Warm-season grasses grow more in the warm part of the year, but have good ability to root more deeply and explore a larger soil reservoir; accordingly their ability to tolerate drought is greater.

When establishing your lawns, it may be worthwhile discussing your needs with a local nursery or turf specialist. Remember that what you need is a functional lawn, not a perfect bowling green. Don't create a high-maintenance demand for yourself by choosing a grass that needs lots of 'TLC'.

Consider planting native grasses instead. Many of these are very beautiful, and are now more widely available from native plant nurseries. Rather than a mown sward, you will have delightful tufty growth that can be augmented by the use of native shrubs. Furthermore, they are generally grasses that grow most during the winter when water is more readily available, and less in the summer, ensuring a lower water demand. They are ideal as an adjunct to a native plant garden.

How and when should you water?

Poor watering practices lead to water waste. Do a water audit regularly to check the effectiveness of your watering system.

- Design your watering system so that water application patterns do not overlap excessively; once they are implemented, check regularly that the heads do not need adjustment (for example, if some areas dry out, while others remain consistently wet).
- Fix leaks.
- If the water flow is too high, change the existing heads for those with a low rate of delivery.
- Water early in the morning when evaporation loss is least, and wind is less.
- Water deeply and less frequently. This is preferable to frequent short waterings, since the grass will be encouraged to root deeper as the top 2–3 cm dry out. The available reservoir becomes greater and reduces the danger of drought stress. Another advantage is that there will be fewer shallow rooting weeds, mosses and algae as the soil dries out.

Watering frequency is an important issue to be considered. We have seen that the evapotranspiration rate is a significant factor in water loss from soils, and provides an invaluable basis for watering frequency. Other approaches may be used, however. One is to automatically control a system, and to water at a regular frequency, say, weekly. While this is low in maintenance it is not necessarily water effective, the water is being applied whether it is needed or not. A water-sensor that overrides the irrigation system may be beneficial: a device that either assesses rainfall and overrides the system, or one that measures soil moisture in the ground. Above-ground devices to record rainfall at a specific location must be so placed as to obtain an average measurement, while below-ground sensors specific to the soil depth and location give information on the water available to plants — they do not indicate the water requirements of the plant. Compare this water information with your own observations.

You may perhaps choose to use your automatic system through the dry season, and simply switch it off during the wet season, only using it in unseasonally dry periods.

Recording rainfall is most important in understanding your garden, and a simple rainfall measuring device attached to a fence is invaluable in your appreciation of rainfall or dryness. Rainfall alone, however, is not the vital issue; wind, orientation, soil type, and so forth, will all have a significant effect on water availability. By developing an appreciation of rainfall you will find out when watering is necessary. You can also take plugs of the soil and assess its moisture content, and thus the need for water.

Grass itself will show its need for water:

- Grass requiring watering will show footmarks after it has been walked over. The grass returns to its previous form only slowly.
- The grass may appear dull, leaves having folded to reduce water loss.

With a manually operated system you can water when these stresses become apparent.

Warm-season grasses	Cool-season grasses
Couch grass and hybrids	Kentucky Bluegrass
Kikuyu	Tall Fescue
Blue Couch	Chewing's Fescue
Buffalo	Perennial Ryegrasses
Zoysia	Browntop Creeping Bent

The warm-season grasses listed have good tolerance of drought, as do the fescues among the cool-season grasses; however, other cool-season grasses are much less tolerant.

Many different cultivars of these grasses are available, and they vary in their qualities. For example, the cultivars of couch Santa Ana, Wintergreen and Greensleeves Park provide a denser cover than couch itself; as its name suggests, Wintergreen retains its greenness in winter bettter than others. Buffalo and Kikuyu produce a rather coarse turf, and the latter can be very invasive, spreading very easily from lawns into garden bed areas especially if smaller whipper-snippered pieces are left lying on the soil. It also easily spreads from one lawn to another; it will spread fast and invade successfully.

Tall Fescue has good drought tolerance and is probably the best choice of the cool-season grasses, whereas the many cultivars of Kentucky Bluegrass require ample summer water to keep their appearance.

Coring

On heavy soils use a technique called coring, the soil beneath the turf being partly removed in long cores, and the spaces filled by a sandy loam by top dressing (a process that allows the sandy loam to fall into these hollows while also filling depressions on the surface). Water thus moves more rapidly from the surface, giving deeper watering and improved aeration. Such a process is not likely to be needed regularly on the ordinary home lawn, but can be useful on heavy soils.

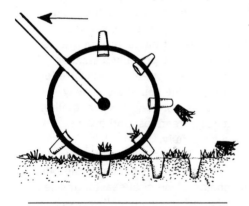

Coring. Plug removed from lawn.

Improved aeration and water penetration

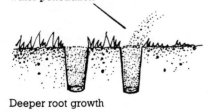

Deeper root growth

Top-dressing replaces soil plug with sand mixture.

Maintenance for your lawn

Maintenance has a significant effect on your lawn's water consumption. The routine procedures of grass maintenance include mowing and fertilising.

Very close mowing of grasses may result in increased evaporation from the soil surface. Scalping (the removal of all the grass to leave the soil surface exposed) results in weed invasion and a poor sward quality. The image of bowling-green lawn shown in so many advertisements creates a false expectation. A longer grass is quite acceptable to most home gardeners, especially since it requires fewer applications of water and fertiliser, as well as less work.

Cool-season grasses may be mown higher. This results in sufficient foliage to encourage a vigorous root system with penetration of a greater soil volume, and thus a greater water reservoir. The tolerance of these grasses to heat also becomes greater, so that they need less frequent water. On the other hand, the greater leaf area may result in greater water loss, and thus a greater water demand, but this is balanced by an improved general appearance because of the fewer weeds and open patches. It is sensible to cut cool-season grasses high in summer, lowering the cut in autumn, and raising it again through the spring. Cut warm-season grasses shorter in the summer, but leave them longer in the winter.

Although removal of grass clippings is frequently advocated, by doing so we effectively remove fertilisers from the soil. We then have to apply fertilisers to replace the nutrients removed. Retain grass clippings with a mulching mower: the clippings fall to the base of the grass, where they effectively reduce evaporation; they also become incorporated into the soil by worms, improving the soil structure and fertility, and water movement deep into the soil.

Where conditions do not suit worms, perhaps because excess fertilisers have been applied or because the soil is too acid, grass leaves could build up as a layer on the soil surface. This layer, known as thatch, can be water-repellent, preventing water entry into the root zone. It may also become a habitat for disease, and can shade out the grass. Remove thatch build-up (over large areas with machinery, or in the home garden with a rake).

Thatch build-up may be worsened by the application of too much fertiliser encouraging rapid growth, an increased water demand and thus a need for more frequent mowing. Don't necessarily apply fertiliser at the levels directed on the pack; only apply sufficient to achieve satisfactory growth as an enhancement to recycled nutrients. If you have a problem with thatch, try to ascertain why. Improve your soil conditions, and try adding worms.

Mowing removes the foliage where photosynthesis occurs, and it is likely that root growth will also be restricted. Water stress may be likely, so this is a good time to water. However, periods of high humidity are times when fungal attack may take place, so avoid cutting the grass and thus creating wounds when the atmosphere is humid. Disease entry is likely to be greatest when wounds are greatest, so your mower blades should be sharpened to cause the least damage to the grass.

To reduce damage to your lawn, avoid cutting grass after rain or irrigation when soils are spongy and most prone to compaction.

Water budget

To establish a watering regime you must take into account the soil type, rooting depth of the plant, the type of growth required, and the evaporation rate of the area. If you know how much water is available and how much your plants use, you will know how frequently you need to water, and the amount. This will depend on the extent of water loss (evapotranspiration, water leached from the soil, wastage during watering) and rainfall. The amount of water available to plants also depends upon how deep and extensively the roots will penetrate the reservoir of soil water, and the type of soil. Study the growth of your plants to decide when to vary watering.

Estimate the volume of soil by assessing the root depth of plants with an auger. For grass it may be 30 cm, for shrubs and trees 50 cm. Calculate the soil reservoir by multiplying the root depth by the volume of water available per cm of soil depth (see Table 1). Then work out how much water is lost by evapotranspiration. Evaporation figures vary Australia-wide (see Table 2, or ask your local meteorological office for figures for your area), and with your micro-climate. Multiply evaporation by a vegetation factor (see Table 3).

Example

In an area of ornamental shrubs growing in a clay soil, in Adelaide, the only growth required is to maintain the vegetative cover of the plant. With a rooting depth of 80 cm, and 1.9 mm of water per cm of soil (see Table 1), water volume will be 152 mm (80 × 1.9). The evapotranspiration factor (see Table 3) is 0.3, so the plant's water loss is effectively 507 mm (152 ÷ 0.3). Assuming daily evaporation is 8.9 mm (typical for Adelaide in January), there is sufficient water for 57 days (507 ÷ 8.9).

This calculation method is suitable for large areas of one plant type, or for a consistent root depth (e.g. massed trees and shrubs). Table 4 gives frequency of watering for different plant types in different soil types. Note that if low growth rates are acceptable, you can extend periods between waterings.

By selecting water-saving plants, considerable savings can be made.

Examples (December in Perth)

- In a loam soil with a low growth-rate requirement, assuming a rooting depth of 50 mm, the water reservoir is 100 mm (50 × 2.0).
- For a plant with low drought tolerance, with evaporation at about 8.7 mm/day and an evapotranspiration factor of 0.7, the available water is 143 mm (100 ÷ 0.7). If evaporation is 8.7 mm, plants must be watered every 16 days (143 ÷ 8.7). By contrast, the evapotranspiration factor for drought-tolerant plants will be 500 mm (100 ÷ 0.2). With evaporation at 8.7 mm, plants must be watered every 57 days (500 ÷ 8.7).

Table 1 Approximate amounts of water that can be removed from soils, at field capacity (see page 19), to maintain plants at different conditions

(Water in mm; soil depth in cm; intermediate soil structure or quality of growth are between).

Plant growth	Sand	Loam	Clay
Lush	0.3	0.9	0.7
Moderate	0.5	1.7	1.3
Minimum	0.6	2.0	1.9

(Figures based on Handreck & Black, *Growing Media for Ornamental Plants and Turf*)

Table 2   Evaporation rates (mm per day)

	Sydney	Melbourne	Adelaide	Perth	Brisbane
January	7.5	7.6	8.9	9.3	6.3
February	6.7	7.0	8.2	8.5	5.3
March	5.5	5.1	6.2	6.9	4.9
April	4.5	3.4	4.2	4.3	4.1
May	3.2	2.0	2.7	3.1	2.9
June	3.0	1.4	2.0	2.3	2.4
July	3.2	1.6	2.0	2.4	2.6
August	4.0	2.3	2.7	2.8	3.6
September	5.1	3.2	3.9	4.0	4.6
October	5.8	4.4	5.6	5.6	5.3
November	7.1	5.5	6.9	7.1	6.3
December	8.7	7.0	8.4	8.7	7.0

Table 3   Evapotranspiration factors

Lawn grass

Cool season:	Lush	0.8
	Moderate	0.7
Warm season:	Lush	0.6
	Moderate	0.3

Ornamentals

Vigorous during establishment, water-demanding	0.7
Moderate, some drought tolerance	0.4
Minimum, desert plants	0.2
Vegetables, fruit trees	0.7

Table 4   An easy guide to days between watering

Lawn	Sand	Loam	Clay
>35°C	1	3	4
30–35°C	1	4	5
25–30°C	2	5	6
20–25°C	3	5	7
15–20°C	4	6	8

Vegetables and flowers			
>35°C	1	2	3
30–35°C	1	2	4
25–30°C	2	3	5
20–25°C	2	4	5
15–20°C	3	5	6

Native and introduced plants			
>35°C	3	7	10
30–35°C	4	7	15
25–30°C	4	10	15
20–25°C	7	10	20
15–20°C	10	15	30

(Figures from Hardie Pope, *Easy Guide to When Should I Water*)

Watering systems

Watering systems apply water to soil even when there is no natural rainfall. In determining the amount of water required, you must take into account aspects of the site: soil type, existing rainfall and its seasonal pattern, whether luxuriant and productive growth is required (e.g. for vegetables and annual display plants) or whether plants (such as native plants) need only sufficient water to survive during drought.

Before you install a watering system consider how the natural rainfall can be used effectively for maximum benefit: soil conditions should be suitable to absorb rainfall, and the design of the garden should allow water to be collected and used on site. This aspect of design is vitally important in Australia's drier areas.

Harvest your rainfall

In some areas, such as parts of Western Australia, evaporation often exceeds rainfall, and can be ten times greater than the annual average rainfall. If you have no supplementary water, you must choose plants that will survive and grow on sporadic rainfall and reduce their water demand throughout dry periods.

In other places, like Melbourne, water is available as rainfall for much of the year; additional watering is only required in drought seasons or at the end of summer when high temperatures and hot winds have dried the soil. By harvesting water you can capture any rainfall falling on the site and use it on your site before doing any supplementary watering. This is not easy to do in a small sub-divided unit garden but has considerable benefits for larger urban-fringe blocks or in blocks where rainfall is exceptionally low. This should be part of an overall philosophy of site development as it reduces the need for supplementary watering. Water harvesting in a small city garden could be achieved by a paved area sloping towards a garden bed or lawn so that available water runs into these areas. Consult the table of water infiltration rates: water infiltrates different soils at different rates — a clay soil moves the water more slowly than a sandy soil. It matters little whether the water remains within the root zone of plants, it will move down through the site, eventually recharging underground aquifers.

Opportunities for water harvesting are greater on a large site:
- Slightly dish lawn areas to provide a water-retaining bowl.
- Slope driveway and car parking areas towards grassed areas.
- Design a swale (shaping the ground to form an open, sloping-edged drainway) to carry much of the excess water into the dam for future use.

In the driest areas, where water is extremely seasonal, treat the whole site as a catchment area and collect water from roof surfaces and paving. Allow the

Watering points:
- Watering is most efficient at night when there is a reduced evaporation rate.
- Water at a rate to match the rate of passage into the soil.
- Deliver water where it is required, not over paved areas.

Infiltration rates

The rate at which water enters the soil is most important, since it reflects the rate of rainwater and any supplementary water entering the soil. There is no point in you watering at a rate quicker than infiltration, as it may run off, especially on slopes where infiltration rates are slower. The figures in the table show the value of creating dishes in sloping sites to hold the water and ensure effective penetration.

Soil texture	Infiltration rate (mm of water per hour)	
	Flat ground	Sloping ground
Sand	20	8
Sandy loam	7	3
Clay	5	2

(Figures from K. Handreck, *Gardening Down-Under*.)

Water harvesting

In northern Western Australia it is estimated that 30 mm of summer rainfall is required to stimulate growth of plants. A rainfall of 5 mm would be too low, but, if collected over an area of, say, 6 square metres of paving, a square metre of planting will receive a total of 30 mm of water. There may be some loss through evaporation, but the value of water harvesting is very clear. Karratha (WA) received 11 weeks of rainfall between 1982 and 1986 — by water harvesting on this 6:1 ratio this could have been increased to the equivalent of 27 weeks, an increase of 250%.

This technique is useful elsewhere. Between 1981 and mid-1986 Perth could have achieved a 770% increase (from 7 weeks to 54 weeks — the period for which a 30 cm depth of dry sand would have been wet outside the main winter rainfall season).

rainfall to fall directly from the roof onto planted areas, or to be carried to ground-level by spouts or gutter chains to well-mulched planted areas. On clay soils allow water to soak in through gravel-filled trenches; top large gravels with a dressing of more attractive river-washed pebble.

A rainwater tank can be an ideal means of holding reserves of water. When you are releasing large amounts of water onto garden beds, be careful this does not cause erosion.

Water harvesting is more efficient if it is used in association with other techniques:
- Mulch the soil to a sufficient depth that will allow the soil to remain open to accept water.
- Prevent compaction of wet soils to allow water percolation.
- Retain existing vegetation to retain root structure in the soil and the associated build-up of organic debris.
- Apply gypsum to soils if your tests show this will be beneficial.
- Apply composts to improve soil structure and pore size.
- Remove thatch from lawns, and assist water penetration by aeration.

Watering systems

A survey of watering systems in Bendigo and Melbourne showed six broad approaches: handwatering by hose (42%), moveable sprinkler systems (48%), fixed sprinkler systems (3%), micro-sprays (2%), drip irrigation (2%) and other techniques (e.g. watering cans) (4%). It is likely that fixed sprinkler systems, micro-sprays and drip systems will be used more frequently as the message of efficient watering becomes widespread, and as lawn watering systems become less expensive.

Watering efficiency

To check that your watering system is efficient, and to know how much water is supplied:
- Place empty food cans in a regular grid on your lawn around your sprinkler system.
- Turn the system on and allow it to run for a couple of hours.
- Then measure the depth of water in each can.
- Take the average reading to find out the average amount of water delivered. If there is a large difference between the highest and lowest reading, adjust your system to prevent dry spots.

	Advantages	Disadvantages
Hand-held hose There are a number of attachments to hoses (e.g. hand guns) for different uses. Many watering systems fit to the end of a hose. These have the great advantage of being mostly low cost, and because of their lack of mechanical parts they last a long time.	• A hose, even with a tap fitting and spray attachment is inexpensive. • Hand watering keeps you in touch with your garden, and able to notice any outbreaks of pest damage and weeds. • You can water specific items. • It is a water-sensitive method (you are unlikely to water during or after rain).	• Hand-watering is time-consuming. • Because it is tedious, light (shallow) waterings are more likely, leading to shallow roots. • Delivery rates, and therefore run-off tend to be quite high, and erode mulches and soil. • There is no measure of the volumes of water supplied. • It does not suit turf areas or groundcover areas; and foliage may prevent water reaching the ground. • Summer watering often takes place during daylight, and significant evaporation can occur.

ABOVE: *Anthemis cupaniana*, a coreopsis, *Achillea* 'Moonshine' and a pink-flowered yarrow create the character of a traditional border, with little water. (PHOTO: JOHN PATRICK)

RIGHT: Plants grouped together in a garden should have similar water demands. This group of laurel, echium and shrubby honeysuckle receives no supplementary water, and all co-habit comfortably. (PHOTO: JOHN PATRICK)

BELOW RIGHT: With careful selection, you can have a traditional herbaceous border. The plants should all be able to tolerate dry conditions, as in this border at Heronswood (Dromana, Vic.). (PHOTO: JOHN PATRICK)

Paving should complement the style and mood of a garden. These native plants are suited to the outer zone of the garden where paths can be informal and surfaced with mulches, with plants blending into the paving. (PHOTO: LANDSCAPE AUSTRALIA)

	Advantages	Disadvantages

Rotating-head systems

Rotating or whirling watering equipment consists of a rotating arm device, or an impulse type of head or a spinning baffle device, all of which apply water in a circular pattern. Their rate of coverage varies, the impulse type covering a larger area, but more slowly than do the quite rapidly rotating arms and baffles.

Advantages
- Price varies from quite inexpensive devices to more expensive sophisticated equipment.
- Best on relatively flat ground.
- The equipment is easily moved to other parts of the garden.

Disadvantages
- Water distribution is not always even within the area of throw; equipment must be moved.
- The lightweight equipment is easily knocked over.
- Generally used during the day when evaporation and wind are greatest.
- The throw is usually circular, leading to water wastage at the edge of paths, etc.
- No automatic control over watering time; dependent on the skill and knowledge of the operator.

Oscillator sprays

These popular systems are readily available.

Advantages
- Very stable.
- A wide throw in a generally rectangular pattern: an even water distribution at a medium rate of water application, allowing water to soak into soil.
- Because of high throw can be used over a wide range of plant types.
- Adjustable.

Disadvantages
- The high throw results in a significant wind blow and relatively high evaporation.
- You have to assess when to move the equipment, so watering will be during the day when evaporation is high.

Water tractors

These tractors are very popular.

Advantages
- An extended area of relatively level ground can be watered without constant attention.
- The medium rate of application and movement of the equipment allows good water penetration.

Disadvantages
- Needs relatively level ground.
- Wind blow and evaporation likely, especially during the day.
- For lawn use only.
- Uneven distribution of water, with concentration at the centre.
- Not very effective on long grass.

Fan sprayers

These stationary devices give a fan spray of restricted extent.

Advantages
- Relatively inexpensive, simple to use, no moving parts.
- Can be moved to any location.
- Useful for shrubs and groundcovers.

Disadvantages
- Some evaporation, and wind movement can change watering patterns.
- Uneven distribution, heavier at the edges, corners not covered.
- Requires constant attention.
- Much of the water is applied high on the plant, leading to wastage and fungal disease problems.

Soaker and perforated hoses

A range of perforated hoses is now available, including the new leaky pipe varieties. Though these materials are designed to be moved, they are best when left to water a particular area over an identified season.

Advantages
- Relatively inexpensive.
- Little evaporation; water is applied close to ground level.
- Useful for watering long rows.
- Can be controlled on timers, and applied at night.

Disadvantages
- Perforated hoses are easily damaged, and puncturing may lead to different rates of water application.
- Uneven water distribution.
- Care is needed to ensure that the quantity of water supplied is adequate.

	Advantages	Disadvantages
Flood systems	• Useful for new plantings in dished areas.	• Some evaporation. • Erosion can be a problem. • Not for general use.
Fixed-head systems — pop-up heads These watering systems, now used more extensively, are more sophisticated in controlling water application. Pop-up sprinklers are often used for lawn areas, in conjunction with drip systems or micro-sprays.	• Designed for specific garden areas, with a number of stations. • Different areas of throw from a choice of heads that can be fine-tuned to allow for wind movement and rainfall. • Damage is minimised by underground pipes, and solar breakdown is limited. • Heads are retractable below ground level. • Different duration and frequency settings are possible. • Automatic control systems allow evening and night-time watering.	• Expensive to install, especially with sophisticated automatic timers and water sensors. Best controlled by skilled and qualified contractors, but this is more expensive. • Needs maintenance; on large sites this is complicated. • Digging trenches may damage existing vegetation. • Existing mature trees may impede effective watering. • Potential water loss by evaporation. • Foliage of shrubs and groundcovers may develop fungal problems.
Fixed system with micro-sprays	• Relatively inexpensive, and simple to implement. • Automatic or manual control linked to timers (not usually to sensors). • May be operated more frequently to meet demands in particular micro-climates, such as for areas of full sun. • Can be located beneath foliage of larger shrubs to ensure water reaches root zones. • Trenches unnecessary; pipes can be laid on the soil surface and protected by mulch.	• Will clog without a suitable filter, which must be cleaned. • Subject to breakage and damage to surface pipes. • Subject to evaporation and wind blow. • Not suitable for lawn areas.
Drip systems These systems are becoming increasingly popular.	• A recent survey found that 21 per cent of gardeners used this type of system once a week or less, a reflection of its value for slow, deep watering, particularly overnight. • Cheap. • Easily constructed. • Efficient use of water, without susceptibility to wind or evaporation, delivers required amount of water directly to the root zone. • Automatic control, suited to sensors and inexpensive timers. • Salt in the water is carried to the outer part of wet zone from the dripper. • Liquid fertilisers can be applied through the system. • Dry areas between drippers may inhibit the growth of weeds. • Suitable for slopes; the slow application is unlikely to cause erosion. • 'Spaghetti' piping can be added to link the system to containers, hanging baskets, etc.	• Pipes can be damaged during weeding. • Restricted root growth if watering is not long and deep. • The small dripper heads can become blocked; they need regular cleaning, and a good filter. • Water may reach areas beneath established shrubs and trees where it is of only very limited benefit.

Mulching will save water

A mulch is a layer of material placed on the surface of a growing medium, generally soil, for:

- weed control
- modification of temperatures
- reduction of evaporation
- improved appearance
- improved soil structure (often only in the long-term as mulches break down)
- improved water penetration
- where a crop is being cultivated, a clean crop.

Some materials make better mulches than others, some are better for some purposes than others. Choosing a mulch is often a compromise: balance effectiveness with visual appearance and, of course, availability and cost.

Weed control

Weeds use water in exactly the same way as ornamental plants. Some weeds won't thrive in dry conditions, but in general weeds will thrive under the same conditions as ornamental plants.

The ability of mulch to suppress weeds depends largely on the depth of the mulch. By preventing light reaching the ground, mulch reduces germination. If germination does take place, the seedlings will generally be thin and leggy, and quite easy to remove from the loose mulch.

If the mulch cover is too deep (especially those mulches that pack down, such as sawdust), this may prevent water penetration to the soil and, perhaps more importantly, oxygen reaching the roots of ornamental plants. This will inhibit their growth. Mulch should be no more than 5 cm deep.

Some perennial weeds, rooted in soil (e.g. couch, nutgrass and kikuyu) can grow through mulches. Apply herbicides on an ongoing basis to control these weeds before you mulch.

Some mulches, especially organic mulches, introduce weeds. There is nothing more frustrating than finding yourself with weeds you didn't have before. Shredded tree prunings, for example, may contain the seeds of trees such as *Ligustrum* sp. (Privet) or *Acer negundo* (Box Elder). Straws (pea, oat or barley) may seem to be a problem, but don't worry too much about the resulting crop, as the seedlings are very easily pulled out. Homemade compost also provides seedlings (mine has given me melons and tomatoes).

Mulches providing a seed-bed for weed growth because of their fine texture and their water-holding capacity are more of a problem. Mushroom compost will enrich the soil, but weeds germinate readily in its surface.

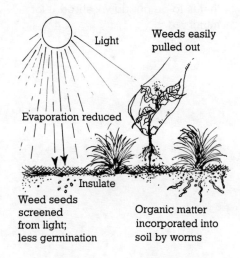

Mulches contribute to water conservation in many ways.

Clean crop

Home-grown vegetables are now popular, but sometimes crops that bear at ground-level, such as strawberries and zucchini, can be prone to mildews, etc. Straw is the ideal mulch beneath these plants, not only to save water but to ensure clean produce.

Mulches

It is always possible you may find an excellent mulch locally that is not generally available. Many mulches are waste materials, and much of their cost derives from the cost of transporting them. You may save money by collecting this material yourself. It may be worthwhile contacting local tree surgeons who shred felled brash, for this makes excellent mulch and it may otherwise be tipped for landfill.

If you have a tree on your site that is to be cut down, shred it for mulch.

Trees

Use plastic sheeting as a mulch around trees in grass areas to prevent competition from turf grasses. Add an organic mulch over the plastic for an attractive visual effect. Once the tree is established (say, in two or three growing seasons), remove the plastic.

Modifies soil temperature

Mulches help control the temperature of soils, and this will affect growth. In mid-summer heat the soil under a mulch will be surprisingly cool and moist; the mulch acts as an insulator, reducing soil temperature.

Black plastic mulches raise the soil temperature throughout the year. Clay soils remain cold in spring, delaying plant growth, but plastic mulch boosts early growth by increasing temperature. High summer temperatures will increase transpiration and water use and, with continued heat, will kill roots. A sensible strategy is to use plastic mulches around newly established young plants in spring to ensure maximum growth, then cover them with an organic mulch as summer temperatures rise.

The problem with many mulches, but especially black plastic, is that plant roots grow close to the surface where oxygen is available. Even when organic mulches are used on their own, the roots may be drawn into the moist cool soil immediately below the mulch. Remember that deep rooting is beneficial in helping plants to survive drought.

Reduces evaporation

Mulches reduce evaporation of water from the soil surface, not only because the surface is shaded but because the mulch slows wind movement across it. As water evaporates, more water is drawn to the surface. This process will continue unless the column of water movement is broken by mulch.

Mulch can reduce evaporation from bare soil by 60 per cent.

Plants can act as living mulch: they shade the soil surface, act as windbreaks, and reduce evaporation and weed growth, even if at the same time they take water from the soil and transpire it into the atmosphere.

Visual effect of mulches

The selection of a mulch by how it looks depends on personal preference. Mulches will change colour as they are exposed. A new mulch of eucalyptus chips, for example, will go grey with time, so even though the reddish colour may at first clash with the colours of your brick paving or building it will soon mellow to a most acceptable harmony. The most attractive mulches are dark-coloured (e.g. fine shredded pine bark, or mushroom compost), a fine foil to the colour and shape of foliage.

In native plant gardens it is really effective to use a dressing of mulch like the floor of native woodland, with eucalyptus clippings, fern foliage, etc. Gravels look good in cottage gardens, especially for paths where naturalised bulbs and other plantings grow through the gravel to soften the edges of paths; gravels and granitic sands team well with succulents. Sometimes mulches can be major elements of a garden design: gravel paths, for instance, or large cobblestones used as a mulch with emergent plants.

Some organic mulches are untidy (e.g. pea or cereal straw or lucerne hay), but they are excellent where herbaceous plants grow through and cover them, especially as this encourages the naturalisation of young seedlings. As the mulch encourages soil fauna (e.g. worms), birds enjoy tossing the mulch around in their search for food, creating a problem for tidy-minded gardeners.

Plastic and newspaper mulches do tear, and ragged ends of plastic sheets poking through layers of mulch are unsightly — don't use plastic in home gardens, except in particular circumstances (e.g. when planting trees in lawn). Newspaper, on the other hand, is an excellent mulch, for it breaks down into the soil. Lay it down several sheets thick, and wet it thoroughly before covering it with a more attractive mulch. It is easy to plant new plants through newspaper, but exceptionally difficult to do it through plastic.

Improves soil structure

By adding mulches that break down into the soil you help sandy soils to hold water and improve water drainage through clays. Some mulches, such as seaweed and mushroom compost, rot down very quickly. Use them as soil conditioners, cultivating them into soils before planting. Mushroom composts can be alkaline and high in salts, however, so ask about their suitability before using them.

I prefer mulches that don't break down too fast but add humus to the soil. Pea and barley straw, and the like, break down slowly and build up a splendid humus content in the soil; this assists in water holding.

Plants such as lupins or broad beans can be sown to provide organic material to be hoed into the ground to improve soil structure, as well as adding nitrogen to the soil, and controlling weeds. This is a good approach to follow where you are building a house on the site and you want to leave the garden until later. At the end of the growing season cultivate the green mulch into the soil. It achieves two objectives: breaking up any compaction of the soil, and increasing its organic content.

Lush organic mulches, such as lawn clippings and animal manure, add nutrients to the soil. Both can add weed seeds. Bacteria breaking down sawdust and other woody mulches may make nitrogen unavailable to plants; this problem is overcome by adding ammonium nitrate at a rate of 50 g per square metre.

Leaf litter is a great mulch. In the past this was burnt, but as most local authorities have now forbidden this practice, the leaves can be added as a mulch to the soil surface.

Improves water penetration

Whatever mulch is applied, the soil should be moistened beforehand. It is perhaps advisable to wait for good spring rains before applying mulch, to ensure that the soil is well wetted first.

When heavy rainfall falls on bare, loose soils, especially on sloping sites, soil erosion becomes a major problem. The presence of plants or mulches absorbs some of the energy of water droplets, and mulches hold the water and help prevent erosion.

Thick layers of lawn clippings and sawdust mulches may become hydrophobic: water is repelled, not absorbed. Water may also be absorbed in the mulch rather than penetrating the soil and reaching the plants.

Compost

You may have already established a compost bin. Good compost is so well broken down that it doesn't provide a huge amount of mulch (I use mine as a soil conditioner as required). As your garden matures, add domestic compost as a mulch; and, of course, there will also be more brash available from the

Pruning technique

Prune only as necessary: to remove dead wood, diseased material, and any crossing and rubbing branches, for better flowering, and to remove dead flowers. Tip-prune to retain the required form and density of a plant, but avoid heavy or drastic pruning that will be of little benefit in saving water.

Nitrogen levels

Many food scraps, waste from fresh vegetables, animal manures and leaves contain high nitrogen levels; woody materials and straws are generally low in nitrogen. When you have large amounts of prunings, add blood and bone to the bin at the rate of 1 kg for every 50 cm depth of compost material in the bin.

Open bin

In the traditional open-bin system materials are shifted from bin to bin to achieve satisfactory oxygen levels. While this is undoubtedly an effective system, and is still used in many large urban gardens, it has disadvantages in smaller gardens: it occupies a large proportion of space; the compost is open, and may attract rodents and smell unpleasant.

Mulch protects roots from damage.

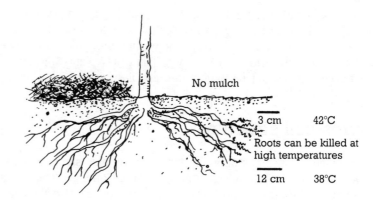

No mulch

3 cm   42°C

Roots can be killed at
high temperatures

12 cm   38°C

Closed bin

The closed-bin system is preferred. Two bins are used, the first filled, and allowed to decompose while a second bin is used. The new Al-Ko Composter has several benefits over the twin bin. It has a basal vent, ensuring an air draft into the base of the compost; internal ribbing carries this air through the bin and prevents the compost from lying against the side of the bin and blocking air movement, essential in ensuring fastest possible breakdown of compost. Slats at the side permit air circulation and form an insulating layer to ensure a consistent temperature. The top of the bin may also be adjusted to two positions to control the speed of airflow. A trapdoor at the base of the bin permits the compost to be removed as it is made.

Rotating bin

A rotating bin gives an excellent compost mix in 8 to 14 days. The greatest problems of rotating bins are their high capital cost and the space that they occupy.

Rotating compost bins speed production.

garden. Drop tip-prunings and other plant debris (foliage and stems from herbaceous plants, hedge and tree clippings) into your compost bin, but be careful not to spread disease.

A good shredder is really useful:
- Hire one, if your garden is small, or purchase one between three or four neighbours, and share it.
- Many councils provide a shredding service for home-owners in an effort to overcome the waste that is tipped into landfill sites.

Good shredders give a readily useable mulch. Avoid diseased material (e.g. rose prunings); hot-compost these or dispose of them.

After three or four years a small garden with an area of lawn and mixed planting will be close to self-sufficiency in mulch. Collect free mulch from council tree shreddings to meet any additional requirements.

Homemade compost

With changing attitudes of local councils to rubbish collection and recycling, in the future every home will have a composting system. Accommodating the bin within the design of the garden will always be a challenge (see page 11).

There are many ways to make homemade compost. (See Allen Gilbert's *No Garbage* in Further reading.)

The essential requirements are oxygen, water and a source of fuel for the compost bin. Even without following any book recipes you will obtain good compost, but the composting will take longer. (My own compost bin accepts all our organic household waste, including waste foodstuffs and all vegetable peelings. To this we add prunings and lawn clippings, and from this we obtain a rich dark compost almost good enough to eat!)

In compost, micro-organisms break down organic matter. To be completely effective they require adequate oxygen (where there is not enough oxygen, say, with very fine materials, the compost will smell, and the process will be slow), and a suitable carbon to nitrogen ratio. If particles of compost are too large they will break down slowly.

If your bin stands on soil, micro-organisms will easily enter the bin. Otherwise, add a layer of soil at the bottom of a new bin or use a layer of compost from an established bin to act as a starter. With a continuous-bin system you do not need to add starter materials.

The contents of the bin should not be too moist. This can happen if large quantities of grass clippings are added or if wet household waste is placed in the bin, but this is easily rectified by adding dry leaves or prunings.

Maintenance for low-water gardens

As with all other garden types, the low-water garden requires maintenance. If you have chosen well you should find that your plants need little maintenance, with an effective watering system they should be sustaining growth rather than producing prolific new growth. In my book, *Great Garden, No Sweat!*, I make it clear that many of the best ways of reducing maintenance arise from the use of an effective design. Many of the Xeriscape principles suit the low-maintenance garden; for example, the use of extended paved areas is low maintenance *and* water efficient.

Watering systems

With your new knowledge of soils and infiltration rates, and the use of water by plants, you should now have an attractive garden without lush growth. You know also that long deep watering is more advantageous than short waterings in producing deeper root systems with excellent drought tolerance.

In spite of this, even when logical decisions have been made about application rates you are still likely to water your garden too much. As gardens become more established, trees and shrubs will seek water from more distant sources. As you do not want these plants to grow fast, very low water-application rates can be sufficient. Be bold, let the soil dry out before watering.

The most susceptible plants are those recently planted, because they do not have deep, established root systems to seek out water reserves. In critical circumstances water these plants. The soil around crop plants, vegetables, fruit trees and annuals should also be saturated to ensure viable crop production, but they should also be fertilised for efficient water use. If there is inadequate water early in their development, fruiting trees will drop their fruit, while onions, melons, beans, corn and aubergine will not develop.

Maintaining watering systems

Drip and trickle systems

The main problems of drip and trickle systems are blockages, especially where fine organic mulches are used. Check your system regularly (say, every six months) and flush it through annually (for about five minutes) to remove any sediment that might have accumulated in the pipe. It pays to assess the performance of emitters on a regular basis rather than waiting to see an area of garden drying because of a faulty emitter. Malfunctions are expensive in terms

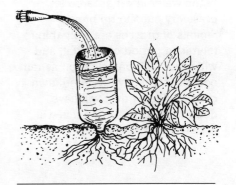

A useful watering device: a plastic bottle with the base removed, and the neck inserted in the ground.

Water down columns encourages deep rooting

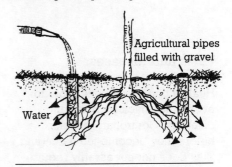

Agricultural pipes filled with gravel

Water

Newly planted tree benefits from deep watering.

Cleaning the heads

Use a thin knife to clean out the offending piece of soil or, if necessary, dismantle and clean the head.

If dirt enters the system when you do this, remove the heads on the station, and run water through until clear.

Drought measures

When water is very scarce let grass dry out and go brown. Stolons of grasses are well able to tolerate a period of drought, and will green up again as soon as rain occurs. If you have watered lawn grasses deeply they will have deep roots anyway, and this will assist in their tolerance.

Pests and diseases

Healthy plants are better able to overcome attack by pests and diseases. Control any attacks before they become too damaging. This does not necessarily require huge amounts of chemicals; use alternatives whenever possible.

of water consumption, and they can also lead to damage, such as root rot and disease, or to worn lawn patches and weed invasion.

My drip systems have suffered extensively from errant forks and spades, but were easily repaired. Mark where the lines of sprinklers are.

Fixed sprinkler systems

Check for leakage, at least monthly, and assess delivery rates annually. Replace any broken sprinkler heads. Water released at an angle is usually the result of a blockage. Clean the filter too: run clean water through annually — do this more frequently if your water line carries a lot of sediment or detritus.

Add more mulch

To continually improve your soil as the mulch is broken down by the action of worms and other micro-organisms, keep adding mulch. I mulch my garden with pea straw after spring rainfall to prevent evaporation of this water. Within a few months most of the pea straw has been incorporated in the soil, and more mulch is needed.

Weed control

Mulches reduce water loss but all plants use water — and that includes weeds. It is pointless to control water loss if weeds are retained in the soil, so remove any weeds prior to planting.

Then remove weeds as they grow. Mulches make it easier to pull them out. With perennial weeds, any remaining little bits of roots will re-shoot; use herbicides to control the weeds. Weed control is especially important while plants are being established (because the plants have the least root volume they are susceptible to drought). Lawn grass can be a weed around the base of newly established plants, so remove it, and dish the soil at the base of new plantings to direct water to their roots.

Fertilising

You do not necessarily want to encourage vigorous new, water-demanding growth. Most well-established larger plants obtain adequate fertiliser by root exploration. Only in exceptional circumstances (e.g. after fire has damaged a tree) will you find it necessary to apply fertiliser. In other circumstances there may be a need for a trace element (e.g. iron on an alkaline soil to make up for a local deficiency), but on the whole avoid extensive nitrogen application because of the lush growth it generates.

Annual display plantings and vegetable crops may require some fertiliser to achieve the best results, but if you don't want to grow the biggest and best you can restrict fertiliser applications.

Pruning

Some people consider that pruning will reduce the water demand of a plant; that, by removing foliage, transpiration and water demand are reduced. Pruning, however, has no effect on the roots, and these continue to supply water. Rapid, vigorous growth is more likely after pruning, together with increased transpiration.

Low-water plants

The following lists give a brief description of some plants suited to low-water gardens. See also other lists throughout this book and in the listed reference books. In future years we will certainly come to know an extended range of native plants. We already grow many low-water plants: a water-efficient garden does not mean replacing existing plants, but changing our focus.

Each entry gives the botanical name and widely accepted common name, as well as a country or region of origin. Not all plants have a common name. Size at maturity (height × spread) is suggested, but this may vary depending upon the growing conditions and plant spacing.

Growth rates (fast, moderate or slow) and drought tolerance are based upon my observations and experience. Xeriphytic plants have an ability to tolerate drought, and drought-tolerant gardens and landscapes are called Xeriscapes. The Xeriscape logo on plant labels indicates those that will grow with little water.

Trees

Acacia pravissima
Ovens Wattle

NSW, Vic., 8 m × 5 m, fast, E

Large shrub or small tree, adaptable as a windbreak and screen, as well as a coastal plant. Grey-green, triangular and pendulous foliage. Excellent tolerance of frost and a range of soils. *Cultivar:* 'Golden Carpet'.

Allocasuarina torulosa
Forest Oak

E. Australia, 20 m × 10 m, fast, E

Elegant foliage, deeply fissured brown corky bark and reddish-brown flowers; excellent in thickets and as a windbreak. Foliage of some is almost

purple in colour. Tolerant of any soils, but needs effective drainage.

Angophora costata
Smooth-barked Apple

S.E. Australia, 20 m × 15 m, moderate, E

The bark peels off to reveal bright orange or pink young bark. The twisted branches produce delightful shadow patterns. White flowers in large quantities.

Arbutus unedo
Irish Strawberry Tree

Ireland, Portugal, Spain, 7 m × 9 m, slow, E

Brown and glossy bark, pendant urn-shaped flowers; round, orange, edible

fruit (both may be on the tree at the same time). May develop an extensive basal root buttress, and will sucker from this if subjected to fire or other stress.

Arbutus unedo (Irish Strawberry Tree) simultaneously bears pendulus white flowers and attractive, edible red and orange fruit.

Celtis australis
Nettle Tree

N. Africa, S. Europe, Middle East, 15 m × 10 m, fast, E/D

This tree has a densely foliaged, broad-spreading canopy on a short trunk; insignificant flowers and small fruit. Provides good shade, and is tolerant of a wide range of soil types, to wind, drought and heat. Birds spread the seed, and it can become a weed.

Ceratonia siliqua
Carob

Mediterranean, 10 m × 10 m, slow, E

Outstanding ability to tolerate drought. Foliage is of glossy, dusty green leaflets; insignificant flowers, followed on the female plant by long pods.
A rather spreading shrub, but occasionally exceptionally sized specimens are encountered. It can be pollarded effectively.

Chamaerops humilis
Mediterranean Fan Palm

S.W. Europe, 6 m × 4 m, slow, E

A beautiful spreading palm for the smaller garden with several rough trunks and strongly shaped leaves.

Cordyline australis
Cabbage Tree

NZ, 10 m × 3 m, slow, E

Grows in most soils, tolerates cold and heat, flood and drought. Sword-like leaves and masses of cream flowers; the purple leaf form is used as a short-term bedding plant. Excellent in containers.

Cupressus glabra
Arizona Cypress

S.W. USA, 15 m × 10 m, fast, E

Blue-grey foliage, extreme drought tolerance and ability to withstand sun and hot winds, grows well without irrigation.

C. macrocarpa
Monterey Cypress

Coastal California, 20 m × 10 m, fast, E

Scented scale-like evergreen foliage; a columnar young tree, spreading with age. Forms a fast-growing hedge, an effective windbreak and screen. Regular clipping is essential. Dislikes poorly drained soils.
Cultivar: 'Aurea'.

C. sempervirens
Italian Cypress

W. Asia, Mediterranean, 15 m × variable, fast, E

This species is quite variable. It is exceptionally tough, with an excellent drought tolerance; greyish foliage when young maturing to a dull grey-green.

Elaeagnus angustifolia
Russian Olive

W. Asia, 6 m × 4 m, slow, E

Scented small yellow flowers, silvery grey foliage.
Good drought-resistant qualities.

Eriobotrya japonica
Loquat

China, 7 m × 8 m, moderate, E

A useful fruiting tree where water is restricted, leathery leaves strongly ribbed above and woolly below. Masses of scented white flowers producing panicles of yellow, pear-shaped fruit. A rather lax growth, which makes it difficult to use in formal garden settings.

Fortunella margarita
Cumquat

China, 5 m × 4 m, moderate, E

Glossy dark green leaves; oval orange-coloured fruit. Can be cultivated as a container plant. It prefers a well-drained soil, and dislikes heavy conditions.

Geijera parviflora
Wilga

NSW, Qld, Vic., 6 m × 8 m, fast, E

Tolerant of arid areas. Its wide spreading canopy is not suited to smaller gardens. Pendant linear leaves. Useful for extended windbreak planting and as a fodder tree, especially in drought.

Melia azederach var. australasica
White Cedar

NSW, NT, Qld, WA, 20 m × 12 m, moderate, D

With its broad canopy, a most useful shade tree. It is suited to an extensive range of Australian habitats. It has excellent drought tolerance, though some supplementary water ensures a faster growth rate and more luxurious canopy. It has glossy and dark green leafy foliage; lilac flowers; globular yellow fruits, which are poisonous.

Olea europaea
Common Olive

Mediterranean, 6 m × 5 m, slow, E

Staple food tree, especially in the Mediterranean. Foliage grey-green above, silvery below; slow to break down on the ground. Small white spring flowers; fruits are largest with suitable irrigation.
Cultivars: 'Barouni', 'Manzanillo', 'Sevillano', 'Verdale'.

Washingtonia filifera
Californian Fan Palm

S.W. USA, 20 m × 5 m, moderate, E

A stocky trunk and a mass of fern-like fronds. It requires space to be fully appreciated. Not tolerant of heavy clay soils, preferring a more open, sandy soil. It absorbs as much water as possible during wet conditions, and is then able to tolerate extended heat and drought.

Shrubs

Abelia × grandiflora
Glossy Abelia

Garden hybrid, 2 m × 2 m, moderate, E

Excellent when massed; arching branches. Flowers late spring to autumn; mauve bracts in winter. Tolerant of a wide range of soils, but needs supplementary water on sands.

Alyogyne huegelii
Blue Hibiscus

SA, WA, 2.5 m × 3 m, fast, E

Needs full sun, effective drainage, and a frost-free site. Masses of soft mauve hibiscus-like flowers. Short-lived in cooler areas or on heavy soils, and can lack root stability. Tip-pruning lengthens its life, giving a denser plant.

Banksia spinolosa
Hairpin Banksia

NSW, Qld, Vic., 3 m × 5 m, moderate, E

Showy golden flowers with purplish-black contrasting styles. Relatively low tolerance of waterlogging, but will tolerate some shade (e.g. beneath an established eucalypt canopy). A fine feature plant. There are a number of excellent dwarf variants.

Callistemon 'Harkness'

Cultivar, 5 m × 4 m, fast, E

Enormously showy bright scarlet-red flowers; young foliage has a delightful pink tinge. Its density of foliage makes it an excellent windbreak and screen, and as a softening element against fences. Benefits from tip-pruning for dense foliage.

Calothamnus quadrifidus
Common Net-bush

WA, 3 m × 4 m, moderate, E

Characteristic one-sided flower spikes provide excellent colour throughout the summer. Good tolerance of coastal situations and heavy soils, though it prefers open drainage; tolerates a low-water regime for an extended period.

Cassia artemesioides
Silver Cassia

W. NSW, N. SA, 2 m × 1 m, fast, E

Finely pinnate grey leaves and bright yellow flowers. Requires good drainage and sun, but will grow in filtered light. Tip-pruning is desirable if it becomes leggy. A plant of outstanding textural quality when set against darker foliage backgrounds.

Eriostemon myoporoides
Long-leaf Wax Flower

NSW, Qld, Vic., 3 m × 2 m, moderate, E

This is my favourite native shrub, a superb plant with an outstanding form. Large white flowers, contrasting with the pink buds; dense flowering. Good drainage is essential, but the plant prospers in a wide range of conditions: shade to full sun, open sands to clays. It has an excellent ability to tolerate drought. Prune when cutting flowers. Five sub-species and numerous cultivars.

Escallonia macrantha
Common Escallonia

Chile, 3 m × 3.5 m, fast, E

Glossy serrated, deep-green leaves and rose-pink flowers. Tolerates shade and dry conditions. It clips well as an evergreen hedge, a fine foil to more detailed planting.

Euphorbia wulfenii and *Convolvulus mauritanicus* are two popular low-water plants of contrasting character. Both are good weed suppressants, and enjoy a sunny position.

Euphorbia characias ssp. wulfenii
Shrubby Spruge

Greece, Turkey, 1.8 m × 2 m, moderate, E

Excellent foliage form and structure, variable blue-green; flowers with bold heads; some enormous. Excellent drought tolerance; it also has the capacity to seed itself into crevices.

It requires full sun; aged branches must be removed to allow new season's growth.

Indigofera australis
Australian Indigo

Australia, 1.5 m × 1.5 m, moderate, E

Dark greyish-green foliage and pale purple to lilac pea flowers (excellent against silver foliage). Prefers full sun and open soil, but will tolerate some shade and heavy soil. Should be tip-pruned even as a young plant to retain density. It is very variable because of its enormous distribution range.

Leptospermum rotundifolium
Round-leaf Tea-tree

NSW, 2 m × 2 m, moderate, E

A tight ornamental growth habit; flowers vary from white through creams to pink and purplish pink, a good cut flower. Tolerant of an extensive range of habitats, including a range of soils and climates, coastal exposure, light shade and extended drought.
Cultivars: 'Jervis Bay', 'Julie Ann', 'Lavender Queen'.

Melaleuca wilsonii
Wilson's Honey Myrtle

SA, Vic., 3 m × 4 m, moderate, E

Numerous mauve-pink flowers through spring and early summer. Tolerates extremely dry conditions, flooding, frost, semi-shade and full sun. Tight growth is retained by regular clipping; it is particularly useful as a hedge.

Nerium oleander
Oleander

Mediterranean, 4 m × 5 m, moderate, E

A thoroughly drought-tolerant plant, grown as a small tree, a hedge, slope reinforcement and a screening mass.

Remove ageing stems from ground level, especially when scale and sooty mould develop in extremely dry situations. Flowers vary from white through rose-pink to deep pink; best as single colour masses.
Note: all parts of this plant contain a highly poisonous milky juice.

Phebalium lamprophyllum

NSW, Vic., 1.5 m × 1.5 m, moderate, E

A neat small shrub with elliptical leaves, densely covered by small white flowers in spring. Plant in full sun or shade. Maintain the tight form by light pruning after flowering. It tolerates dry shade and some frost.

Raphiolepis indica
Indian Hawthorn

S. China, 3 m × 3 m, slow, E

Remarkable tolerance to dryish shade. Leathery, toothed leaves and clusters of showy pink spring flowers; purple-black berries persist on the plant for several months but are very poisonous.

Zauschneria californica
California Fuchsia

California, 300 cm × 500 cm, moderate, E

A sub-shrub with a woody stem base producing arching stems. Grey green foliage with red flowers at the end of the stems. They are outstanding for their toughness and their ability to grow in any soils, providing they are planted in full sun. Prune to ensure dense growth. The species is very variable in flower colour and form.
Cultivar: 'Albiflora'.

Climbing plants

Campsis grandiflora
Chinese Trumpet-creeper

China, moderate, D

The large red tube of the trumpet creeper flower is one of the showiest of the climber flowers. It has fern-like leaves, but because it does not produce aerial roots it must be supported on a wall.

Jasminum polyanthum

China, fast, E

Prolific flowers and foliage; it produces masses of wiry stems unless trained and pruned. Fern-like foliage; perfumed white flowers with reddish-purple tubes.

Podranea vicasoliana
Pink Tecoma

South Africa, moderate, E

The fern-like foliage may be deciduous in cold areas. Perfumed tube flowers, pink with darker pink veins. This is not too vigorous, and can be kept tidy and neat on an arbour or climbing frame.

Tecomaria capensis
Cape Fire Flower

South Africa, moderate, E

Bright scarlet flowers in winter and spring. It is an exceptionally vigorous plant; without suitable pruning it will form a dense, coarsely wiry messy shrub, with extensive branching leading to masses of suckers, but it can be trained on fences and over water tanks.

Groundcovers

Acacia cultriformis '**Australflora Cascade**'
Knife-leaf Wattle

NSW, Qld, 300 mm × 3 m, moderate, E

Outstanding drought tolerance. Yellow spring flowers. The normal form of this plant grows to 5 metres, but this cultivar is excellent as a spreading shrub, best when falling over a retaining wall or growing in a large container. It requires drainage, but is otherwise tolerant.

Convolvulus mauretanicus
Blue Morning Glory

N. Africa, 150 mm × 750 mm, moderate, E

Masses of bright-blue funnel-shaped flowers. With full sun it flowers consistently, even through winter. It has good salt tolerance, but dislikes foliage being too wet.

Osteospermum ecklonis is one of the many South African daisies well suited to groundcover use in low-rainfall areas.

Gazania splendens
Gazania

South Africa, 150 mm × 300 mm, moderate, E

Most effective in masses. Dark-green foliage with a silver reverse; large daisy flowers, mostly orange, yellow and brown, that open in the sun but close up in cloudy days and at night. Enormously tolerant, growing in a wide range of soils and with a minimum of supplementary water.

Grevillea juniperina (prostrate form)

NSW, prostrate × 2 m, moderate, E

A variable plant. It may grow to 4 metres, make an excellent hedge and windbreak; as the foliage is prickly it may not be ideal for every location. The prostrate form gives a dense groundcover, ideal for extensive use. Red flowers throughout the year; attractive to birds. It will tolerate some shade, wetness, diverse soils and some frost, but may need clipping to maintain shape.

Helianthemum nummularium
Rock Rose

Europe, incl. Mediterranean, 150 mm × 600 mm, moderate, E

A woody sub-shrub with masses of small flowers (white, pinks, reds, oranges, yellows, with bright yellow stamen eyes) throughout the summer; narrow linear foliage, often grey-green and covered with fine hairs. It needs sun for flowering, and dislikes shade. A little supplementary water helps. Lightly prune at the end of the season for a tight plant form. Re-establish the plants with young material every five years.

Sedum spectabile (Ice Plant) produces flowers in varying shades from cool through to darker pink. It is a great butterfly attractant.

Lasiopetalum macrophyllum (prostrate form)

NSW, Tas., Vic., prostrate × 3 m, moderate, E

A variable plant; upright growing forms provide effective screening and windbreak plants, the prostrate form is a useful groundcover for semi-shaded positions beneath trees and shrubs. It also has outstanding coastal tolerance. The misty cream cupped flowers in spring are attractive to birds.

Myoporum parvifolium
Creeping Boobialla

NSW, SA, Vic., prostrate × 3 m, fast, E

Beautiful foliage covers the ground tightly over extended areas; it bears pretty white flowers. It is a most tolerant plant, best in open soil in full sun but will grow in shade when the canopy is opened up a little; will also grow in clays.

Grey foliage plants

e = emergent; g = grass;
gc = groundcover; p = perennial;
s = shrub; t = tree
Drought tolerance: *** (high)
               **, * (good)

Acacia cultriformis	s	***
A. pendula	t	**
Artemisia arborescens	s	***
A. ludoviciana	s	**
A. schmidtiana	gc	**
Cassia artemesioides	s	***
Cedrus atlantica f. glauca	t	*
Cerastium tomentosum	gc	*
Chrysanthemum ptarmiciflorum	s	*
Convolvulus cneorum	gc	*
Cupressus arizonica	t	***
Echeveria imbricata	gc	**
Elaeagnus angustifolia	t	*
Eucalyptus cinerea	t	***
E. kruseana	t	***
E. polyanthemos	t	**
E. sideroxylon	t	**
Festuca ovina glauca	g	**
Guichenotia macrantha	s	**
Helleborus argutifolius	p	**
Juniperus chinensis 'Pfitzeriana Glauca'	s	**
Leucophyta brownii	s	**
Lychnis coronaria	p	*
Olea europaea	t	***
Pereskia atriplicifolia	s	*
Santolina chamaecyparissus	s	*
Senecio haworthii	gc	**
Stachys byzantina	gc	*
Teucrium fruticans	s	***
Westringia fruticosa	s	**
Yucca whipplei	e	*

Plants for containers

b = bulb; gc = groundcover;
p = perennial; s = shrub; t = tree
Drought tolerance: *** (high)
               **, * (good)

Agapanthus praecox ssp. orientalis	b	**
Argephyllum frutescens	s	**
Cineraria maritima	p	**
Clianthus formosus	s	**
Convolvulus mauritanicus	gc	*
Euphorbia biglandulosa	gc	***
Fortunella marginata	s	**
Helichrysum petiolare	p	**
Laurus nobilis (clipped)	t	**
Nandina domestica	s	*
Olea europaea (clipped)	t	***
Pelargonium cv.	p	**
Scaevola crassifolia	s	**

Plants with attractive bark

Drought tolerance: *** (high)
               **, * (good)

Angophora costata	**
Arbutus menziesii	***
Eucalyptus caesia	*
E. citriodora	**
E. maculata	**
E. sideroxylon	***
Lagerstroemia indica	*
Pinus halepensis	**
Quercus suber	**

Plants with outstanding foliage

s = shrub; t = tree
Drought tolerance: *** (high)
               **, * (good)

Acacia dealbata (divided)	t	**
Aucuba japonica (variegated)	s	**
Berberis thunbergii 'Atropurpurea' (purple)	s	*
Caesalpinia gilliesii (finely divided)	s	**
Cassia artemisioides (needlelike grey)	s	***
Cotinus coggygria 'Royal Purple' (purple)	s	***
Dodonaea viscosa (bronze)	t	**
Elaeagnus pungens 'Maculata' (variegated)	s	**
Koelreuteria paniculata (divided)	t	*
Limonium perezii (large roundish leaves)	t	**
Lophostemon conferta 'Variegata' (variegated)	t	**
Nandina domestica (divided)	s	**
Osmanthus heterophyllus 'Variegatus' (toothed, white-edged)	s	**
Robinia pseudoacacia 'Frisia' (divided, gold yellow)	t	*

Palms and palm-like plants

Drought tolerance: *** (high)
               **, * (good)

Beaucarnea recurvata	**
Chamaerops humilis	**
Cordyline australis	**
Dracaena draco	***
Phoenix canariensis	***
Trachycarpus fortunei	*
Washingtonia filifera	**
W. robusta	**

Fruiting plants

Drought tolerance: *** (high)
               **, * (good)

Citrus limon	*
C. × paradisi	*
Diospyros kaki	*
Eriobotrya japonica	**
Feijoa sellowiana	*
Ficus carica	**
Fortunella margarita	*
Olea europaea	**

Bulbs

Drought tolerance: *** (high)
               **, * (good)

Allium christophii	**
Cyclamen coum	**
Freesia refracta	***
Gladiolus communis subs. byzantinus	**
Iris unguicularis (rhizome)	***
Muscari armeniacum	**
Narcissus papyraceus 'Paper White'	*
Nerine sarniensis	**
Tulbaghia violacea	**
Tulipa clusiana	**

Neil Marriott's garden shows that native plants can be combined for beautiful effects of texture and colour.

Further reading

Brookes, J. *Gardens of Paradise: The History and Design of the Great Islamic Gardens.* Weidenfeld & Nicolson, London, 1987.

Brookes, J. *Your Garden Design Book: The Complete Practical Guide to Planning, Styling and Planting Any Garden.* Lothian, Melbourne, 1991.

Burnett, J. & Leake, S. *Making Your Garden Grow.* Lothian, Melbourne, 1990.

Crocker, C. (ed.). *Gardening in Dry Climates.* Ortho Books, San Ramon, California, 1989.

Eckersley, R. & Stafford L. *Living in the Garden, Australian Style.* Lothian, Melbourne, 1993.

Elliot, W. R. & Jones, D. L. *Encyclopaedia of Australian Plants*, vols 2–6. Lothian, Melbourne, 1980–93.

Gilbert, N. *No Garbage.* Lothian, Melbourne, 1992.

Greig, D. *The Australian Gardener's Wildflower Catalogue.* Angus & Robertson, North Ryde, NSW, 1987.

Handreck, K. *Gardening Down-Under: The Handbook for Enquiring Gardeners.* CSIRO, Melbourne, 1993.

Handreck, K. & Black, N. *Growing Media for Ornamental Plants and Turf.* University of New South Wales Press, Kensington, NSW, 1986.

Harris, R. W. *Arboriculture: Integrated Management of Landscape Trees, Shrubs and Vines.* Prentice-Hall, Englewood Cliffs, New Jersey, 1992.

Latymer, H. *The Mediterranean Gardener.* Frances Lincoln, in association with the Royal Botanic Gardens, Kew, 1990.

McKinnon, M. *Arabia: Sand, Sea, Sky.* BBC Books, London, 1990.

Melbourne Water Resources Review. *Interim Report: Water for Our Future.* Melbourne Water, Melbourne, 1992.

Oehme, W. & van Sweden, J. *Bold Romantic Gardens: The New World Landscape of Oehme and van Sweden.* Lothian, Melbourne, 1990.

Patrick, J. *Designing the Small Garden.* Lansdowne, Sydney, 1994.

Patrick, J. *Great Garden, No Sweat!* Lothian, Melbourne, 1994.

Patrick, J. *Trees for Town and City Gardens.* Lothian, Melbourne, 1990.

Perry, R. *Landscape Plants for Western Regions.* Land Design Publishing, Claremont, California, 1992.

Robinette, G. O. *Water Conservation in Landscape Design and Management.* Van Nostrand Reinhold, New York, 1984.

Sunset Books. *Waterwise Gardening.* Lane Publishing Co., Menlo Park, California, 1989.

Taylor, J. *The Dry Garden: Gardening with Drought-tolerant Plants.* Lothian, Melbourne, 1993.

Wilson, G. *Landscaping with Australian Plants.* Nelson, Melbourne, 1975.

Index

NOTE: Plant names listed in the grey panels throughout this book are not included in this index.